War and the Christian Conscience

War and the Christian Conscience
Where Do You Stand?

Joseph J. Fahey

ORBIS BOOKS

Maryknoll, New York 10545

Founded in 1970, Orbis Books endeavors to publish works that enlighten the mind, nourish the spirit, and challenge the conscience. The publishing arm of the Maryknoll Fathers and Brothers, Orbis seeks to explore the global dimensions of the Christian faith and mission, to invite dialogue with diverse cultures and religious traditions, and to serve the cause of reconciliation and peace. The books published reflect the views of their authors and do not represent the official position of the Maryknoll Society. To learn more about Maryknoll and Orbis Books, please visit our website at www.maryknoll.org.

Library of Congress Cataloging-in-Publication Data

Fahey, Joseph.
  War and the Christian conscience : where do you stand? / Joseph J.
Fahey.
       p. cm.
  Includes bibliographical references.
  ISBN-13: 978-1-57075-583-5 (pbk.)
  1. War—Religious aspects—Christianity. I. Title.
  BT736.2.F334 2005
  241'.6242—dc22
                                  2005012360

To three combat veterans
who had the courage
to follow their consciences:

ROY BOURGEOIS

CHARLIE LITEKY

HUGH THOMPSON

And to people young and old
who must do the same

Contents

PART III
WAR AND YOUR CONSCIENCE

Acknowledgments

So many people inspired and helped me with this book. First, I should acknowledge students and faculty colleagues, principally from the Religious Studies Department and the Peace Studies Program at Manhattan College. I have taught my students variations of each chapter for years and they have been very helpful in telling me what to emphasize or what to leave out. So thanks, dear students!

Some of this work was completed while on a sabbatical from Manhattan College. In addition, my colleagues at Manhattan College have also helped me in so many ways that the mere mention of their names does not begin to do them justice. These colleagues both inspired and helped me: Michael Antolik, Robert Berger, F.S.C., Seamus Carey, Pamela Chasek, Tom Ferguson, Tamara Fish, Don Gray, Margaret Groarke, Lois Haar, Stephen Kaplan, John Keber, Luis Loyola, Judith Plaskow, John Barry Ryan, Luke Salm, F.S.C., Michelle Saracino, Claudia Setzer, Catherine Shanley, Andrew Skotnicki, O.Carm., and Mark Taylor. Thanks all.

Through the years, colleagues and friends in the Consortium on Peace Research Education and Development, the Peace Studies Association, Pax Christi, the Christophers, the Catholic Theological Society of America, the Fellowship of Reconciliation, and other associations have provided both inspiration and advice. To mention only a few of these wonderful people: Richard Armstrong, Elise Boulding, Louis M. Brown, Drew Christiansen, S.J., Larry Colburn, Tom Cornell, Dorothy Day, Richard Deats, Eileen Egan, Valerie Flessati, Bill Frazier, M.M., Joe Grassi, Tom Gumbleton, Bryan Hehir, Dan Hallock, Connie Hogarth, Mike Hovey, Vic Hummert, James Keller, M.M., Bruce Kent, Bill McCarthy, M.M., Dick McSorely, S.J., Rev. Andrew Murray, Ronald G. Musto, James O'Connell, Betty Reardon, Paul Rogers, Pete

Seeger, Gene Sharp, Walter Sullivan, Gerry and Janice Vanderhaar, Peter and Cora Weiss, and Gordon Zahn.

It has been very helpful to consult military sources and Web sites to understand both the "law" and "ethics" of war. Special thanks to Archbishop Edwin F. O'Brien of the Archdiocese for the Military Services, USA and his staff for guidance in locating manuals that instruct soldiers on the laws of war in combat operations. I am also grateful to Colonel Daniel Zupan of the United States Military Academy who provided valuable assistance on just war materials. The *Army Times* and other military journals have helped me understand how soldiers view the matter of conscience and war. Visits to the Pentagon, West Point, Ft. Benning, the Navy War College, Parris Island, and other military bases through the years have also been helpful. I have found that professional military officers view war in much more realistic terms than do their civilian commanders, who often see it as an abstraction, or in purely political terms, or even as an ideal.

I am deeply grateful to my colleagues Michael Antolik, Drew Christiansen, S.J., Richard Deats, Michael Hovey, Catherine Shanley, and Andrew Skotnicki, O.Carm., who offered critical and constructive comments on several chapters. My son Michael, my brother Tom, and my sister Jacqueline Schaaf read the manuscript and were very supportive. Friends Patricia Casey, Fr. Ron Cioffi, and Joann Vitalo also read the work and offered very helpful comments. Many thanks for the guidance and patience of Robert Ellsberg, Sue Perry, Celine Allen, the wonderful people at Orbis Books. Regrettably, I have not been able to follow everyone's advice, thus any omissions and mistakes are very much my own.

I am deeply indebted to the work of the many fine scholars whose insights are reflected in these pages (see "Sources Consulted" at the end of this book). I am particularly grateful to Dr. Ronald G. Musto for his outstanding contributions to the field of Christian peace scholarship. His numerous books and publications were extremely helpful to me and, in fact, many of the primary sources I have quoted are from Ron's books.

This book is dedicated to three people I am privileged to call friends. Roy Bourgeois is a U.S. Navy veteran and Maryknoll priest who has labored, in and out of jail, to close the School of the Americas and to reform U.S. policy in Latin America. Roy continues to inspire many to stand for justice. Charlie Liteky is a former U.S. Army chaplain who received the Medal of Honor in Vietnam and has since been jailed for his opposition to U.S. policies, especially in Latin America. In 2003 Charlie traveled to Iraq to urge U.S. soldiers to resist the war. Hugh Thompson is a U.S. Army veteran who stopped the massacre at My Lai and has since called on every soldier to respect the rules of war and the mandate of conscience. Each man rose above his culture to demonstrate to all of us that true courage is faithfulness to one's conscience in the midst of considerable adversity. These men are models of conscience and this book is respectfully dedicated to them.

Introduction

This is a book intended for the general reader who may never have personally decided where he or she stands on war.

In your heart of hearts, where do you stand on war? Are you willing to kill other human beings? Are you willing to be killed? Would you be willing to send your children off to kill or be killed? Would you encourage others to go to war when you don't? Do you think war is a moral or an immoral human activity?

Writing after the devastation of World War II, French philosopher Albert Camus thought it important that people should make a choice between either "being murderers themselves" or "refusing to do so with all their force and being." That is, on such an important issue that threatens the lives of millions, one cannot sit on the moral fence of passivity, or indifference, or ignorance. In this age of weapons of mass destruction, one simply cannot remain morally neutral about military service or the institution of war. Conscience is demanded of us all.

Through my years of teaching and lecturing I have found that many people mistake their culture for their conscience. They think they should follow the views of their nation, or their religion, or their family. I have discovered that very few people have ever seriously examined the issue of war and come to their own personal decision with regard to it. War for many is an abstraction, even an ideal. War evokes the chivalry of the medieval knight and the heroism of those who shed their blood for the "fatherland." In the words of the title of a recent book by Chris Hedges, "war is a force that gives us meaning." Because it is seen either as duty or as destiny, war is something that is hardly ever examined from the perspective of conscience. And, interestingly, a great many people assume that Christianity has always accepted war as an ethical enterprise.

Of course, as a teacher I have the opportunity to go into some depth on the subject of war and the Christian conscience and I constantly deal with students who tell me they have never seriously thought about war. Although the young men, in particular, register with the Selective Service at the age of eighteen, they rarely think about actually going to war. Instead, they register to avoid the consequences of the loss of student loans, or the penalty of fines, or social ostracism. But few young men—or women—have *any* convictions about war, and their schools and parishes teach or preach next to nothing on the Christian conscience and war.

So young people are left adrift in a sea of ignorance and indifference. Some of them even go to war without knowing why they are doing so. As time goes by and young people move into middle age, they still don't really know where they stand on war. Many even grow old and die without ever having known where they stood on war.

This book is an attempt to help the reader examine where he or she stands on war. First, we examine the complex nature of conscience. We look at how it is defined and consider seven major perspectives that form conscience: culture, duty, egoism, gender, religion, science, and utilitarianism. Textbooks on ethics generally mention only a few of these perspectives; we have included them all in order to offer as comprehensive an approach as possible.

We then move on to examine four major "models" of conscience with regard to war: pacifism, just war, total war, and World Community. (These models are presented in the order in which they were developed through the course of Christian history.) Most discussions of war and conscience limit themselves to only two models, pacifism and just war, but it is essential to include total war and World Community, first, because they actually exist in Christian history, and second, because each has its advocates today. It is clear that Christianity does not speak with one voice on the morality of war.

The reader should not give in to the temptation of reading only the chapter that promises to be most appealing. For how does one really know where one stands unless other perspectives or models are considered? Many people I encounter, for example, actually subscribe to a total war model but mistake it for a just war position. In addition, many people who reject pacifism think the only other option is war, when in fact a World Community approach may be more satisfactory.

Since this is a book directed at a popular audience, notes and extensive reading lists have been left out to make the book as readable and short as possible. The final section of the book lists the sources I consulted in writing each chapter. But this listing should be understood to be the tip of a rather large iceberg that includes numerous encyclopedias, scholarly journals, and other reference sources.

Throughout this book I have tried to use material that is in the public domain or that is commonly used by scholars and authors. Also, wherever possible, I have allowed the historical "actors" in the drama of war and peace speak for themselves. What better way is there to understand the past than to invite great historical figures to repeat their words in our own time?

The Swarthmore College Peace Collection is an invaluable source for anyone who is researching a book of this type. In addition, hundreds of Web sites have been consulted and the amount of information available in an instant would have been unimaginable just ten years ago. However, the reader will note that very few Web sites are cited. This is because a simple entry like "pacifism" or "just war" in any search engine will bring up thousands of Web sites that will amplify and illuminate almost any subject in this book.

Because of its inclusive translation and excellent notes, *The New Oxford Annotated Bible,* third edition (New Revised Standard Version) has been used for all scriptural quotations. Biblical scholars will undoubtedly point out that the way scripture is used in this book very much resembles the discredited "proof text" methodology that lifts a quotation out of context to twist it to mean something else. There is some truth to this, since I have tried to include quotations and interpretations that are actually used by proponents of each of the four models to justify or explain their positions on war. Where possible, however, for the sake of accuracy, I have noted that all scholars may not accept a particular interpretation of a given passage. This approach illustrates the problem that vexes all who rely exclusively on a biblical interpretation of war and peace matters: isolated texts can prove almost anything. Christian traditions and churches that employ scholarly methods to understand the Bible, however, offer a far more accurate picture of the real meaning of disputed texts.

Every attempt has been made to use inclusive language in this book. Some of the original quotations, however, use masculine forms and, out of respect for textual accuracy, these quotes have been left unchanged. It is important to remember that the first three models—pacifism, just war, and total war—were primarily developed by men. While we assume that women must have been involved in significant ways, the documentary evidence is either not there or has been lost. Women have, however, had considerable influence in the development of the World Community model, both as activists and scholars.

Finally, I have tried to personalize the highly complex historical material covered in this book by introducing a fictional student, Nicole. I have in fact, however, over the course of my lifetime met thousands of "Nicoles" and taught hundreds of classes like the one that follows in "Nicole's Conscience." It has been a joy to see students approach the issue of conscience and war with an open mind and a questioning spirit. I hope the reader will do the same.

PART ONE

Conscience

Nicole's Conscience

President Hunter's announcement stunned Nicole.

"Because of our nation's commitment to spread freedom and democracy to such nations as Iran, Venezuela, Burundi, Cuba, Uzbekistan, North Korea, Columbia, and Syria," the president stated, "I shall ask Congress to pass a law reinstating a military draft for all Americans beginning on their nineteenth birthday. In order to strengthen our national security and to ensure our nation's ability to engage in preventive warfare, I intend to sign this law as soon as possible." The president continued, "There will be no exemptions to this draft. Women as well as men will serve. College students will report for basic training at the end of the semester after their nineteenth birthday."

Nicole was eighteen and a first-year student in college. Until last night's presidential announcement, she had hardly paid attention to the news. She had been much too busy working on her term papers and figuring out which courses to take next semester.

When she woke up this morning, Nicole realized that there would be no next semester; this time next year she would be in the military, perhaps in one of the countries the president had mentioned last night. She realized she had never even *thought* about war before. Nicole was frightened and angry. "Why can't I finish college? Why do *I* have to go?"

On further reflection, Nicole realized that she had no moral position on war. "Where do I stand on war?" she wondered.

Nicole looked forward to her class that afternoon on "Religious Dimensions of Peace." Discussions with her classmates during the morning hadn't helped much, since people were really upset at the thought of being drafted and nobody seemed to have a clear sense of how to respond to the news.

In her religious studies course, Professor Collins had been discussing the fifth-century debate between Pelagius and St. Augustine on original sin. Among other matters, Professor Collins had asked the class to think about whether waging war is an essential aspect of human nature or contrary to it.

The moment class began, Nicole raised her hand and asked, "Professor Collins, can we discuss the announcement the president made last night?" A ripple of sound filled the room as her classmates murmured in agreement.

"Obviously the subject has relevance for us in this course," said Professor Collins. "What's on your mind?"

"I have a lot of questions," stated Nicole. "The first of them is: Why do I have to go? I don't even know where I stand on war."

Professor Collins looked around at the thirty students in the class. Every single one of them seemed to be paying very close attention. So he turned to Nicole and said, "Okay, Nicole. I can see that you reflect the concern of just about everyone in this class. Why don't we sit in a circle and have an open discussion on the issue? Who would like to start?"

Defend your country...

Kate was the first to speak. "Well, even though I hadn't given the issue much thought until last night," she said, "it seems pretty simple to me. We don't really have much choice. We have to be willing to defend our country and our American way of life. If we're real patriots we'll serve in the military..."

"Hold on!" said Nicole. "I'm not sure it's so simple."

"Oh yes it is," said Kate. "Look, Nicole, the United States is the greatest country in the history of the world. No country has ever had as much freedom, opportunity, and prosperity as ours. We have to defend the American way of life against people who refuse to believe in freedom and openness. If we love our country, we will join the military and protect what we have for our children and grandchildren."

"I disagree," Ryan said. "Kate, what you're saying, in essence, is that we have to kill for the American culture or 'way of life,' as you call it. I prefer to think of myself as part of a global culture and to envision global citizenship for all of us. I'm willing to 'go,' but as a member of the Peace Corps or as a United Nations volunteer. Our patriotism should be to the entire world."

It's your duty...

"Sounds good," said Billy, "but each of us still has a duty as citizens to serve our country. And our duty now is to heed the president's call to serve in the armed forces. I trust the president, since he knows more than I do about those who threaten our way of life." Billy paused for a moment, and then he concluded: "'Duty, Honor, Country' is the motto of West Point. It's mine too."

"Billy, you have one thing right," said Harriet. "We do have a duty. But our real duty is to follow our conscience. Remember what Thoreau said? 'Must we ever resign our conscience to the legislature?' Of course not. We should never do anything out of blind obedience; we should serve in the military only if our conscience calls us to do that. If it doesn't, we should refuse to serve."

Think of yourself...

"You have a point, Harriet," said Gregory. "But I think the real duty people have is to think of themselves in any decision they make. We should each ask ourselves, 'What's best for me?' and then we'll know what we should do in any situation." Melanie added: "I agree completely. We should let our feelings guide us. We'll know when something is good for us if it feels good or if the outcome is good for us. We each have a responsibility to think of our own happiness first. When I think about being drafted, it's clear to me that joining the military will not make me happy. How about the rest of you? Do you really want to die—or kill another person—at the age of nineteen?"

"But that is pure selfishness," said Sandra. "If each of us thought only of ourselves we would become a society of narcissistic people who lack any sense of social responsibility. Who would defend children and the weak against attack? We need to think of our country first. And, after all, the Army's slogan does say, 'Be all that you can be.' By serving your country you'll serve yourself. Plus, if you die defending your country, you'll go straight to heaven."

You are a woman...

"Wait a minute," Jacqueline said. "Look, Sandra, you are first of all a woman, and women are simply not meant to take life. We are meant to nurture life. Killing is a man's job. I know some women do serve in the military, but very few are actually in combat. Women are neither biologically nor psychologically suited for warfare.

Women are hardly liberated when they become free to kill other women's children. I refuse to be drafted."

"I respect what you say," said Dan, "but you women simply can't have it both ways. You can't say you want to be equal to men and then try to exempt yourselves from defending your country. There are women fighter pilots and women missile officers and they can do the job just as well as men. The future of warfare is not in the trenches like in World War I. The fact is that women can be just as nasty as men and men can be just as caring as women." Then, turning to the others in the class, he said, "Jacqueline is making a sexist argument. We shouldn't buy into it."

Nicole listened carefully to each of her classmates, and every time someone spoke she could agree with that argument. But now she was *really* confused. What was her duty as an American woman? Before she could start sorting out her thoughts, several other classmates added their comments, which only increased her confusion.

You are a Catholic...

Michael was the next to speak. "I'm a Catholic. The Catholic Church permits military service and at times encourages it to defend innocent people. Catholics are not pacifists. If the president calls me to serve, I feel I must obey, because Jesus told us we had to obey Caesar's laws as well as God's. There are many Catholic priests who wear the uniform of their country as military chaplains. There are a lot of Catholic saints who were soldiers. I think serving in the military is a way of serving God."

"I'm shocked at what you're saying," said Barbara. "You make the Catholic Church sound like a military religion! The church happens to have a long tradition of pacifism and there are also Catholic saints who have refused to serve in the military. In any event, the Catholic Church subscribes to just war principles that accept war only as a 'last resort.' And remember, the word 'Catholic' comes before what you really are: a Christian. Jesus taught only nonviolence as the path to salvation. Above all, you should follow him. *Real* Catholics die for their faith, but they never kill others."

War is natural...

"All well and good," said Tom, "but war is natural to human beings—people are naturally aggressive. We have descended from bloodthirsty killer apes and violence is hard-wired in us. Religion, education, and civil laws help to rein in that violence. There is a great deal of historical and scientific evidence that proves I'm right. And the evidence shows that women can be as ruthless and violent as men, so the fact that women can be drafted now is actually a sign of progress. Military service and war have long been considered manly pursuits; it's high time women joined men as defenders of freedom."

"I'm amazed to hear you talk this way," said Jo-Ellen. "You're just plain wrong about human nature. Contrary to what you're saying, human beings are *naturally* nonviolent and we've survived as a species because we have created cooperative societies and because peacemakers have far outnumbered war-makers in history. If you look at the entire span of human history, you'll see that there have been long periods of peace and there have been a lot more peaceful societies than warlike societies. I'm glad you mentioned science, Tom, but it seems to me that your reading of it is much too biased and selective. All human beings are basically peaceful. We're not killers!"

Look at the consequences...

"Listen, let's get practical," said Mary. "What are we really talking about here? Jacqueline, you said you would refuse military service. What do you think the consequences will be? First, your friends and family will probably reject you; second, you'll go to jail; third, you won't get married; and fourth, you'll have let down your country when it needs you. Think of your future! And it's not a matter of being selfish. Think of how many people you'll help by sacrificing your personal desires for the good of others. If you serve, you'll be a hero, and when you leave for war people will put yellow ribbons around trees until you come home. Above all, don't let them call you a coward. Serve your country, Jacqueline."

"Mary's on the right track," interjected Ariella, "but we should look at the consequences of military service from a wider perspective. Historically, soldiers don't serve the common good; they serve special interests. Wars are fought not for the liberation of the many but for the power and profit of the few. Conscientious objectors maintain their own integrity and show that they are willing to suffer and be jailed for their convictions. Someday, when wars are but a distant memory, such people will be regarded as heroes because they suffered so that others might live. Don't go, Jacqueline."

"I'm feeling overwhelmed," said Nicole. "At the beginning of class I didn't know where I stood on war—and now I *really* don't know where I stand. It all seems so complicated." A number of the other students who hadn't spoken nodded in agreement with her.

"This has been a fascinating discussion," said Professor Collins. "I'm impressed by the fact that people were respectful of others' opinions and didn't belittle or insult those with whom they disagreed. A lot of different opinions were expressed. Let's see if we can sort them out."

Turning to the chalkboard, he said, "I think I heard seven different perspectives on how the issue of war should be addressed. I'll write each one down and then put in parenthesis the names of those who spoke to each one."

Professor Collins then wrote the following on the chalkboard:

1. CULTURE — Nationalism (Kate, Ryan)

2. DUTY — Obligation (Billy, Harriet)

3. EGOISM — Self-interest (Gregory, Melanie, Sandra)

4. GENDER — Sexuality (Jacqueline, Dan)

5. RELIGION — Faith (Michael, Barbara)

6. SCIENCE — Knowledge (Tom, Jo-Ellen)

7. UTILITARIANISM — Consequences (Mary, Ariella)

When he had finished writing on the board, Professor Collins faced the class and said, "So, in answer to Nicole's question, we've come up with a wide range of answers. Here we've tried to do a preliminary sorting of those answers based on perspectives." Then, turning to Nicole he said, "Nicole, does this help?"

Nicole stared at the chalkboard and answered, "It does help, because it gives me a lot to think about. But I need a lot more information about all of this, and about the options I really have before I can make up my mind on where I stand and decide what to do."

"Fine," said Professor Collins. "We're going to spend the next several classes discussing these perspectives and other options for Nicole—and for all of us. The seven perspectives are actually ways of looking at any moral issue. Each one of them helps shape our conscience. In our next class, we'll talk about what conscience is, and about the seven perspectives that help shape it.

"The particular issue we're discussing here, though, is war. So, in addition to looking at the seven perspectives in relation to the issue of war, we're also going to examine four 'models' or approaches to war that have developed over the course of Christian history. We'll look at each of them in historical order."

Turning to the chalkboard, he then wrote:

1. PACIFISM or NONVIOLENCE

2. JUST or LIMITED WAR

3. TOTAL or HOLY WAR

4. WORLD COMMUNITY or GLOBAL CITIZENSHIP

"We're going to be covering some very challenging topics," said Professor Collins. "Please come to class prepared and with an open mind!"

He concluded by saying, "The purpose of an assignment is to help you think more deeply about the subject discussed in class. I'm not giving you an assignment today, because the president's announcement affects each one of you directly—so I know you're going to be doing some hard thinking about what we've discussed. As the course proceeds, however, you'll be getting assignments that help you understand conscience and what shapes it, as well as the four models. And," he added, "your final exam will be to explain where you stand on war."

As Nicole got up to go to her next class, she wondered where she would stand on the issue of war at the end of the course. "Wherever I come out on this," she thought, "I hope I have the courage to follow my convictions."

———— • ————

Where do *you*, dear reader, stand on the issue of war?

Nicole's story is a case study designed to stimulate your thinking so that you can use this book wisely to formulate your own convictions on issues of war and peace. Whether you are sixteen or sixty, have you ever considered the question of whether military service is right or wrong for you? Had you been in Professor Collins's class, how would you have responded to Nicole's question?

Put your response in the form of a letter to Nicole. As you work your way through this book, you'll have the opportunity to revise your response in light of what you'll be learning.

Conscience and What Forms It

In this chapter we will discuss (1) the meaning of conscience, and (2) the seven perspectives or "shapers" of conscience that were introduced in our case study.

As was evident in Professor Collins's class, issues relating to conscience can be very complicated. Should one base ethical decisions on culture, for example? On religion? On science? Or should one select the best elements from several of these perspectives?

Finally, are you aware of how *you* make ethical decisions? If you were to map out your conscience, what would it look like? What great causes would you die for? Live for? Kill for? This chapter is designed to help you answer these questions.

Several comments are necessary before we begin.

First, it is very important that you approach each of the shapers of conscience with an open mind. From the very beginning you must realize that you *already* prefer two or three of these perspectives and, therefore, have a bias against several others. Your culture, your religion, your gender, and other factors have already helped shape your moral preferences. All of our actions are based on philosophy, yet very few of us have ever articulated that philosophy. Let us approach the discussion of these shapers of conscience with a genuine sense of intellectual humility and so try to learn from each of them, including those we don't like.

Second, each perspective is advocated by sincere people who believe that their way is the best way to achieve an authentic human existence and a truly human society. Consequently, each perspective contains some truth and can be helpful to you in forming your conscience. There are some people, for example, who *a priori* reject egoism as a source of conscience, since they believe it to be inherently selfish and narcissistic. While egoism can be used for selfish purposes, we do well to recall that in essence it means "self-interest," and who among us would deny anyone the right to pursue her or his legitimate self-interest?

Third, concerning the life-and-death matter of war and peace, it is essential that *everyone* form his or her conscience, whether he or she advocates pacifism, limited war, total war, or global citizenship. There are certain societies that permit an exemption to military service based on a commitment to pacifism. In those societies, people seeking such an exemption are required to prove the sincerity of their position by undergoing an exhaustive process that involves producing a great deal of documentation and the testimony of experts. On the other hand, most nations *presume* that young people are willing to serve in the military—or, to state it clearly, to kill or be killed for their country—and consequently do not require proof of a position of conscience to serve in the military. Although it is not legally required, such a proof has value. For the sake of personal integrity, those willing to serve in military forces should also be able to state—and document—their position.

The Nature of Conscience

The root of the word "conscience" is the Latin word *scientia*, which means "knowledge." Since knowledge can be applied very broadly, we must ask, "knowledge of what?" In the case of the word "conscience," the knowledge referred to has to do specifically with *ethical* issues.

Hence, for example, "conscience" should not be confused with "taste," as in a judgment about the worth of a piece of art or the quality of food. A painting or food may be judged "good" or "bad," but neither is "unethical"; only the artist or the cook may called ethically good or bad! What we call "good" or "bad," whether in relationship to art, or food, or ethics, obviously differs from individual to individual and from culture to culture.

We can define conscience by saying that it is the innate ability to determine the ethics of actions as morally good, bad, or indifferent.

Let's briefly examine two key terms that are found in this definition of conscience.

"Innate Ability." While some people posit that conscience is an "inner voice" or "inner light" that we are all born with, it is much more commonly acknowledged that we are born with a capacity or an ability to form a conscience and that conscience develops in various ways depending on the culture in which we are raised. Hence, for example, a child who is born into an Islamic family will know nothing of Islamic culture if she is removed from it at birth and raised in, for example, a Buddhist family. Any attempt to tell her later in life that she is a Muslim will fail if she has never been exposed to Muslim influences. (She can, of course, choose later to *become* a Muslim, but she was not a Muslim at birth. At birth, every child is simply a human being.)

The fact is that there is no knowledge that is innate to human beings; we are what we *learn* to be and we become what we *choose* to be. Conscience is universal in the sense that *all* human beings are born with the capacity for conscience and *all* human beings develop their conscience as they journey through life. We should not confuse potentiality with act: humans are born with the *potential* to develop a conscience, but at birth they do not *actually* possess knowledge of what is good or bad. That knowledge is acquired through life experience and education.

"Ethics." The root of the word "ethics" is found in the Greek word *ethos,* which means "character." Aristotle (384–322 BCE) believed that the purpose of human life was happiness and that happiness was achieved through a series of good moral actions that were rooted in good habits called virtues. In the opening sentence of his *Nicomachean Ethics,* Aristotle states, "Every art and every scientific inquiry, and similarly every action and purpose, may be said to aim at some good. Hence the good has been well defined as that at which all things aim." As a discipline, ethics deals with identifying what is good, what is of moral value.

Finally, a word needs to be said about the distinction between ethics and morality. As discussed above, the Greek word for ethics means "character." The Latin root for the word "morality," however, is *mores* or "custom." Hence, morality tends to refer to specific religions or customs, while ethics refers to the universal quest for the good life. Although there is clear distinction between morality and ethics, the terms are often used interchangeably.

With this essential information as our foundation, we will now proceed to discuss the seven perspectives that shape conscience:

_____ CULTURE

_____ DUTY

_____ EGOISM

_____ GENDER

_____ RELIGION

_____ SCIENCE

_____ UTILITARIANISM

Note that these perspectives are listed here (and discussed) in alphabetical order rather than in order of importance. The ranking in order of importance is going to be *your* task. Before proceeding, you might want to look over the list and quickly rank each entry to reflect the perspectives that are important to you in making ethical judgments. Next to each one, place a number from 1 to 7, with 1 being the most important. At the end of the chapter, after you have learned more about each perspective, you can then revisit your ranking and decide whether you want to alter it. If you approach the material in this chapter with an open mind and a willingness to learn, you probably will be making some changes. Have fun!

Perspectives That Form Conscience

Culture

Ethical decisions formed by culture are based on a conviction that the customs and traditions of a specific social group can serve as the norm or rule for determining what is morally right and wrong. A "social group" could be a person's biological or spiritual family, ethnic group, or nation state.

Hence, for example, a group's marriage practices (e.g., polygamy, monogamy); its treatment of women (e.g., subservience to men, equality); its manner of treating animals and the environment (e.g., exploitative, reverent); and its dispute resolution system (e.g., mediation, legal action, violence) are all shaped by societal traditions and customs. In addition, it is not uncommon for people in a society to believe that their mores are superior to those of other societies. Many people subscribe to the conviction that "The world would be a better place if only everyone lived like us!" (You might want to list some of the customs and traditions that serve as norms in your own culture.)

Accordingly, the decision to go to war—or to refuse to go to war—can be made according to the customs of a given society. Among the cultural factors that can help form conscience concerning matters of war and peace are:

Class. Class distinctions—especially between rich and poor— have dominated much of human history. People in the "upper" classes have traditionally considered themselves morally superior to those in the "lower" classes and often believed it their duty to govern them as well. Throughout history there have been numerous wars fought as a result of differences in economic and social class. Wars of rebellion have been waged by the poor against an unjust social and economic order established by the rich, while wars of empire have been waged by rich nations to expand their own power and wealth. Much of the opposition to "globalization," for example, is based on a division between "have not" groups or nations and "have" corporations or nations.

Ethnicity. Our world is characterized by distinctive ethnic communities. As mentioned earlier, some cultures hold that their ethical standards are superior to those of people outside their community. Accordingly, they believe they have the right and even the duty to wage war in order to impose their culture on others. Members of the conquered ethnic community may then engage in war (their opponents often refer to this as "terrorism") to oppose the policies or actions of the group in power. Hence, for example, Croats have opposed Serbs, Hutus have fought Tutsis, and aboriginal people have resisted European invaders. Ethnic conflict has a very long history and continues to this day.

Nationalism. Contemporary nation states are "mega" forms of culture that receive allegiance from hundreds of millions of people. National leaders declare war (or send troops into combat) and citizens are expected to support such action as a sign of loyalty to the nation. During times of war, nationalists believe that true patriots must support their flag, their leaders, and their troops. Those who dissent in time of war are thought to be "aiding and abetting" the enemy. "My country right or wrong" is sometimes the motto of the nationalist.

Duty

Ethical decisions based on duty are made in terms of what a person is bound or obliged to do under certain legal or moral covenants. Hence, for example, people are obliged to obey the laws of their country; they are obliged to honor the ethical code of their employer; they are bound to respect professional confidences; they are obliged to follow the orders of legitimate superiors; they are committed to honoring their marriage vows; and they are bound to follow the dictates of their own conscience. (You are invited to make a list of what you perceive as your own duties or obligations.)

Accordingly, the decision to go to war—or to refuse to go to war—can be made in terms of doing one's duty. Among the factors relating to duty that can help form conscience concerning matters of war and peace are:

Law. A law is a regulation concerning human behavior enacted by a government and enforced through police and judicial power. A law is considered just when (1) it is enacted by a legally constituted government, and (2) it promotes the common good. Consequently, one's duty to obey a law is not absolute—there is a long tradition that states: "An unjust law is no law at all." Laws exist at the local, state, provincial, national, and international levels. Hence, when deciding whether to go to war, individuals and states have a duty to ensure that there is a national and international legal basis for military action.

Virtue. A virtue is a moral habit that promotes human happiness. People are considered "virtuous" not because of their adherence to some external regulation or law (as above), but rather because they are of good character and of sound moral integrity. Aristotle tells us that intellectual virtues and moral virtues are formed by good teachers and good habits. In Greek philosophy, the "cardinal" or principal virtues are wisdom, justice, courage, and temperance. In Christian thought, the theological virtues are faith, hope, and love. Virtues determine not just what people *do* but also who they *are* as human persons. Ironically, both warriors and pacifists believe that such virtues as courage, loyalty, and self-sacrifice describe their commitment to defend the innocent.

Justice. Justice is giving to another that which belongs to her or him as a human being. We treat others justly or fairly when we recognize our duty to respect the rights that are inherent in every human being. These rights include just wages, education, honest prices, medical care, political freedom, and defense against injustice. Biblical justice calls for liberation of the poor and oppressed. When one's conscience is shaped by a sense of social justice, one will see such justice, rather than police or military action, as the basis of authentic peace.

Egoism

Ethical decisions influenced by egoism are made in terms of what is in one's self-interest. "What is good for me?" or "How will this affect me?" are the relevant questions. Moral concerns relating to self-interest include, for example, issues having to do with survival, education, health, livelihood, and happiness. A simple question egoists ask themselves is "Am I happy in this relationship... or school, or job, or city?" (You are invited to make a list of those concerns that are most critical to your own self-interest.)

Accordingly, the decision to go to war—or to refuse to go to war—can be made in terms of self-interest. Among the factors relating to egoism that can help form conscience concerning matters of war and peace are:

Happiness. Happiness is a state of serenity that results from following one's convictions and from having found a purpose in life. Egoists believe that every person should be fulfilled as a human being, and that pleasure and joy are essential characteristics of humanity. Enlightened egoists understand, however, that love for oneself often requires giving of oneself to others, especially the poor and powerless. Human beings are social animals: happiness cannot be achieved in isolation from others. Although killing others is difficult for soldiers, some are happy in the thrill of combat while others achieve happiness by defending innocent life or by spreading freedom to other nations. Those who use nonviolence to defend others are happy that they use peaceful means to achieve the goal of peace.

Integrity. People with integrity have the courage to put their convictions into action. The test of a person's convictions is whether he or she is willing to suffer social ostracism, or prison, or death for that which he or she holds sacred. Integrity or "wholeness" means that one gives one hundred percent to one's mission in life. People of integrity don't quit; they persevere until the end. On the part of a soldier, integrity in war demands rigid obedience to the laws of war and the orders of superiors as well as to the dictates of one's own conscience.

Feelings/Intuition. People sometimes state that they did something because they "felt like doing it" or they "just knew" they "had to do it." Emotions are important in ethical decision making, since emotions are essential to full humanity. Moral decisions made without an emotional component are less than whole. The ideal moral decision is made when reason and emotion are balanced in harmony with one another. This balance can be difficult to achieve. It happens all too often, for example, that wars are planned or executed according to strict rational criteria while the suffering of the human beings involved is dismissed as "collateral damage."

Gender

Ethical decisions can be affected by issues relating to gender. Although such issues are complex and there is much lack of agreement about them, there are certainly differences between men and women that result from both biology and socialization. These differences can play an important role in individual determinations of what is morally good or bad.

Accordingly, the decision to go to war—or to refuse to go to war—can be influenced by one's gender. Here are some gender-related issues with regard to war and peace:

Female. Some women regard military service (including combat duty) as a sign of the true liberation of women. Others hold that women warriors violate their nature as mothers and nurturers. Some feminists believe that war is a result of male biology and patriarchy and that it can be ended only when more women move into positions of leadership in the political arena.

Male. Some men regard military service (especially combat duty) as the ultimate expression of manliness or virility. They see the physical and intellectual dominance of men as essential for a secure society. Other men hold that serving in the military is a sign of cowardice, while nonviolence indicates true virility.

Gender issues become even more complex when we consider sexual orientation. The fact is that people can be heterosexual, homosexual, or bisexual. Just as the twentieth century signaled great strides for women's rights, so the twenty-first century may be distinguished by a deeper understanding of the significance of sexual orientation and recognition of the rights of people who are not heterosexual. This will have powerful implications for the conduct of war. For example, there are some countries in which women have been allowed to serve in combat units while homosexuals are barred from serving in any military capacity. Will homosexual (or bisexual or transgender) service in the military be a further sign of sexual liberation? The debate concerning sexual orientation has important cultural, religious, and scientific dimensions and it is certain to continue.

Religion

Ethical decisions can be powerfully shaped by religion, because religion engages people not only intellectually but also emotionally. In addition, religion relates to faith, to what people consider "ultimate good," and is also often directly tied to issues of morality and ethics. Some monotheistic religions hold that the ultimate good is God, who is all-knowing and all-loving and is the Father or Mother of us all. Some theists also hold that God favors one religion over another and will wage war on nonbelievers. Many non-theistic religions hold that there is a purpose to human existence that can be realized by acting in accordance with the harmony of nature or through ethical behavior. Humanists, who reject a supernatural explanation for history, believe that ethics based on science and compassion offers the best hope for human harmony.

Accordingly, the decision to go to war—or to refuse to go to war—can be influenced by religion. Three major expressions of religion that are relevant to matters of war and peace are:

Theistic religions. The three major religions that concern us here are the monotheistic religions—Judaism, Christianity, and Islam. These religions are sometimes known as "religions of the book," since they all base their beliefs on a written source that is rooted in the Bible. The three religions hold in common a belief in a loving God who seeks universal peace. This same God, however, can also be vengeful and violent. All three religions also believe there are evil spirits or demons that can tempt or influence humans to commit sin or violate God's commandments. The struggle between the forces of "light" and "darkness" is for many Jews, Christians, and Muslims at heart a spiritual struggle that can be won only with weapons of the spirit. Others believe that the struggle must be fought in physical terms, through war.

Nature-based religions. Many aboriginal religions and some Asian religions are based on the belief that people are part of nature and can achieve their meaning in life only by living in harmony with the cosmos, the earth, and fellow creatures. Practitioners of these religions believe there is a spiritual unity that permeates all physical reality. That spiritual unity is the source of life and serves as the ultimate destiny for all creatures, including humans. Hence, there is no evil or "sin" as such; there is only ignorance and separation. People are not necessarily more or less evil; they are more or less ignorant or more or less unconnected. Consequently, these religions tend to refrain from killing anything that has a spirit, and that includes animals. Wars are fought for defensive reasons, but warriors are not held in high esteem.

Reason-based religions. Religious humanists believe that humanity is its own highest good and that people can and must save themselves. They do this through the use of reason and the application of science and technology to their lives. Humanists

believe that nature itself explains the mystery of life and the reason for existence. They hold that deeds are more important than
creeds in creating social justice and global harmony. Humanists
tend to be global citizens who believe that economic interdependence and international law will eventually abolish war.

Science

Ethical decisions shaped by science are rooted in scientific knowledge. (We mentioned earlier that *scientia* in Latin means "knowledge.")
As human beings, we know things through sensory experience. Thus
it is possible to measure what we know, to test what we know, and to
communicate what we know. We can use the physical, social, and life
sciences, for example, to determine whether homosexuality is natural
to humans, whether competition is more effective than cooperation,
whether violence is an essential aspect of the human character,
whether government is superior to anarchy, whether war makes peace,
etc. Ethical decisions based on empirical data are derived from experi-
mentation, observation, and experience rather than from theory, or
faith, or prejudice.

Accordingly, the decision to go to war—or to refuse to go to
war—can be grounded in scientific knowledge. Two areas relating to
knowledge that are particularly relevant to matters of war and peace
are:

Natural Law. The theory of natural law states that some laws are
basic and fundamental to human nature. Human beings, using
the power of their reason, can discover these laws and, through
them, determine the proper norms for ethical behavior. Advocates of natural law hold that ethical behavior is *natural* for
human beings, while unethical behavior is *unnatural* for humans. We can discover what is ethical or unethical through education and through an examination of our end or destiny as
human beings. (Atheists believe that our destiny can be understood in terms of natural philosophy, while theists believe that
our destiny must be seen in light of the supernatural.) Some advocates of natural law believe that human nature is *static* or un-
changing, while others hold to a *dynamic* or developmental view
of what it means to be human. Is war natural to humans and is

peace unnatural? Or is peace natural and war unnatural? Natural law can be used to seek answers to such questions, and it does so primarily through scientific discovery.

Education. An educated person is a person who seeks information from as many sources as possible and then makes a judgment about the correct way to behave. Education may be formal, or intellectual (from school) or it may be informal, or experiential (from the school of life). Moral decisions are best made using both intellectual *and* experiential sources. Hence, we can know what is ethical through study of the liberal arts (philosophy, literature, art, etc.), the life sciences (biology, psychology, etc.), the physical sciences (physics, chemistry, etc.), and the social sciences (anthropology, sociology, government, etc.)— as well as through reflection on life experience. A "correct" or well-formed conscience is of necessity an educated conscience. Consequently, education that is based on sound research can contribute to strategies that avoid war and promote the nonviolent resolution of conflict.

Utilitarianism

Ethical decisions shaped by utilitarianism are based on the conviction that the *results* of an act determine the morality of that act. If the results are beneficial (especially to a large number of people), then the action taken to achieve those results may be deemed to be morally acceptable. Stated another way, the ethical value of an action is determined by the worthiness of the consequence of that action or by the benefit that it produces for the majority of people—"the greatest good for the greatest number."

Thus, for example, it may be morally acceptable to amputate someone's arm in order to save that person's life; inferior or unsafe products may be produced if generating wealth is seen as the ultimate value; sacrificing one life to save a hundred may be seen as ethical; or, on a larger scale, the loss of twenty thousand lives in war may be acceptable if one million people are saved. There is, of course, no moral equivalence among these examples, but they do demonstrate the tension between actions and their consequences and highlight the difficulty in answering the question, "What actions are morally acceptable in order to produce the greatest good?"

Accordingly, the decision to go to war—or to refuse to go to war—can be shaped by utilitarian considerations. Here are two ways in which such considerations can apply to matters of war and peace:

Career Ethics. Individuals generally choose professions that are consistent with their conscience and ethical standards. People opt for careers in government, education, business, or the military because they believe these careers will enable them to live morally honorable lives. Conflicts between professional duty and personal honor can arise, however, when people are ordered to violate or ignore standards of professional ethics. In such cases, some people choose to resign, or to speak out, or to be jailed in order to be true to their conscience. Others, however, opt for career over conscience. They look at the check they get each week or month and decide to set aside their judgment of right and wrong in favor of unquestioning obedience to the mandate or mission of the institution that pays their wages. "I was only following orders," is the oft-stated justification for illegal or immoral behavior on the part of a person who follows "paycheck" ethics. "I was only following orders," was, of course, the justification given by many Nazis at war-crimes tribunals after World War II.

Means and Ends. A utilitarian ethic can be strongly pragmatic (practical) in its approach to getting things done. People who are totally committed to pragmatism believe that questionable moral means may be employed in order to achieve a great good or to attain a worthy goal. "The end justifies the means," is their motto. They argue that they are only being "realists" when they tolerate illegal or immoral means to produce good results. In warfare, such people hold that killing innocent civilians is morally acceptable as "collateral damage" if, as a result of the military action, more lives are saved than lost. There are, on the other hand, principled utilitarians who hold that immoral means may never be used to produce a good result. They see "killing for peace" not only as a contradiction in terms but also as a counterproductive philosophy. Most principled utilitarians tend toward pacifism in matters of war and peace, since they consider nonviolence the only acceptable moral method of resisting evil.

War and the Individual Conscience

On the issue of war, most people allow others to do their thinking for them. When a president or prime minister engages soldiers in combat, or when a congress or parliament declares war on another nation or group, an overwhelming number of citizens will usually rally around their flag and allow their leaders to decide for them whom they will hate and whom they will kill. People naturally want to trust that those in charge know what they are doing and are acting correctly. Unfortunately, however, history is replete with examples of leaders who "misled" their nations into unjust wars or wars of conquest.

A grave burden rests, then, on each person to form his or her conscience about war. Citizens who blindly and without question follow the directives of another diminish their core humanity and shirk their responsibilities as citizens. A society is civilized to the extent that it has an educated population that assumes responsibility for the decisions of its leaders.

A civilized society is a society of conscience.

———————— • ————————

Here, once again in alphabetical order, are the seven perspectives or "shapers of conscience" discussed in this chapter:

_____ CULTURE

_____ DUTY

_____ EGOISM

_____ GENDER

_____ RELIGION

_____ SCIENCE

_____ UTILITARIANISM

While reading about each of them, your reactions probably ranged from "Yes, I agree with this" to "This is absurd." You might even have thought, "I'm confused on this one."

Look back at how you ranked them at the beginning of this chapter. Now that you have finished the chapter, rank them once more with the numbers 1 through 7, with 1 being your top choice. Has the order changed?

Next, state reasons why you think one perspective is more important than another.

Finally, challenge yourself by asking why your numbers 5, 6, and 7 rank so low.

This exercise will help form a habit that you can apply to every future moral decision that you will have to make in life.

Recommended Reading

These are some books you might find helpful if you'd like to learn more about conscience and what forms it:

Daniel C. Maguire. *The Moral Code of Judaism and Christianity.* Fortress Press, 1993.

Barbara MacKinnon. *Ethics: Theory and Contemporary Issues.* Wadsworth, 2004.

Louis P. Pojman. *How Should We Live? An Introduction to Ethics.* Wadsworth, 2005.

Scott B. Rae. *Moral Choices: An Introduction to Ethics.* Zondervan Publishing House, 2000.

James P. Sterba. *Ethics: Classical Western Texts in Feminist and Multicultural Perspectives.* Oxford University Press, 2000.

PART TWO

War and Conscience in Christian History

Pacifism

*"The most dangerous element in Christianity,
from the point of view of the established order,
is the refusal to kill a human being."*
Petr Verigin

Introduction

Pacifism is a spiritual and social philosophy that seeks to abolish war and to reconcile enemies through the power of love and the work of social justice.

The word "pacifism" is rooted in the Latin words *pax* and *facere* and it means "to make peace." Hence, rather than "passive" inactivity (as in the mistaken "passivism"), pacifism is an active force that uses social and political power to promote social justice and the unity of nations.

Pacifism rejects hatred, bloodshed, violence, and war as methods of conflict management or conflict resolution. Instead, pacifism employs the hundreds of methods of nonviolent persuasion and resistance that have been universally practiced in human history (but that have only recently been the subject of research). Pacifists are morally opposed to war, since they regard all killing as murder, even if war is legally permitted.

Pacifists may be divided into two groups: absolute or "principled" pacifists and selective or "pragmatic" pacifists. Absolute pacifists are those individuals who object to participation in war in any form. These pacifists are called conscientious objectors (COs). Some principled pacifists object only to killing in war and will, therefore, serve in the military, often as medics or in another noncombatant capacity. Other principled pacifists refuse to pay taxes for war or to participate in any institution that prepares people for war. Selective pacifists are those who object to the morality of a particular war (as in "selective conscientious objector"), or to the use of weapons of mass destruction in war (as in "nuclear pacifist"), or to a draft law that compels military service.

The word "pacifism" is of twentieth-century origin (French: *pacifisme*) and generally refers to conscientious objection to military service. According to the United States Selective Service System, "A conscientious objector is one who is opposed to serving in the armed forces and/or bearing arms on the grounds of moral or religious principles." The right to legally claim conscientious objection to war is relatively recent in human history. In the United States, for example, some COs went to jail in World War I, others went to work camps in World War II, and many performed public service in the Vietnam War. People who have objected to war and bloodshed as a matter of conscience, however, can be found throughout history and in every culture.

Pacifism in the Hebrew Scriptures

In order to properly understand the foundation for peace taught by Jesus of Nazareth, we must place Jesus in the context of his Jewish heritage. Jesus was raised as a Jew, he lived as a Jew, and he died as a Jew. Rather than start a new religion or sect, Jesus sought to reform his own religion through the works of justice and the spirituality of nonviolence. Neither a legalist nor a pessimist, Jesus believed that God's reign was breaking into history and that salvation was possible for all people. A brief discussion of the Jewish concept of peace—especially in the Jewish prophetic literature—will help us to understand the pacifism that Jesus preached and for which he died.

The Jews were, and are, a people for whom peace is a sacred ideal. While war has existed in Jewish life, peace is, nevertheless, at the heart of Jewish history, ethics, and rituals. *Shalom* is the Hebrew word for peace and it means a state of perfect spiritual and physical fulfillment. *Shalom* means liberation from oppression and the restoration of God's reign in human affairs. *Shalom* means security and hope, joy and happiness. Nations that live in *shalom* enjoy not only the absence of war but also the presence of harmony and just relationships. While the concept of *shalom* can be found throughout the Hebrew Scriptures, it is most evident in what is known as the prophetic literature.

Between the eleventh century and the eighth century BCE, the Hebrew prophets attempted to impart to the Jewish people God's vision of the world. Prominent among the eighteen or so prophets are Isaiah, Jeremiah, Ezekiel, Hosea, Joel, Amos, Jonah, Micah, Habakkuk, Haggai, and Malachi. Unlike the popular image of a prophet as someone who *predicts* the future, the Hebrew prophets were much more messengers from God who *challenged* the Jewish people—especially their leaders—to an alternative future, one in which peace was possible if it was based on just social relationships. The prophets saw the world through God's eyes and, because of that, they were often outcasts in their own land who suffered frequent persecution from the corrupt leaders of Jewish society.

Political, economic, and social life in prophetic times was not unlike that in our own: there was corporate and political corruption, the poor and aliens were treated unjustly, and the idols of greed and power replaced worship of the true God. At considerable risk to themselves, the prophets challenged others with God's view of peace, which was founded on the work of community justice. Though the causes of injustice were complex, the message of the prophets was simple: peace cannot be achieved until people walk in the ways of the Lord.

While the prophets can be strikingly negative in tone, their central message is one of optimism and hope. The prophets describe what the world will look like when people behave as children of God. Pacifists through the ages have been inspired by numerous passages that look to a world of universal justice, harmony, and peace. Here are a few examples:

Isaiah speaks of a messianic age where peace and justice shall reign:

> For a child has been born for us,
>   a son given to us;
> authority rests upon his shoulders;
>   and he is named

> Wonderful Counselor, Mighty God,
>> Everlasting Father, Prince of Peace.
> His authority shall grow continually,
>> and there shall be endless peace
> for the throne of David and his kingdom.
>> He will establish and uphold it
> with justice and with righteousness
>> from this time onward and forevermore. (Isaiah 9:6–7)

The prophet Micah predicts a period of universal peace:

> In the days to come
>> the mountain of the Lord's house
> shall be established as the highest of the mountains,
>> and shall be raised up above the hills.
> Peoples shall stream to it,
>> and many nations shall come and say:
> "Come, let us go up to the mountain of the LORD,
>> to the house of the God of Jacob;
> that he may teach us his ways
>> and that we may walk in his paths."
> For out of Zion shall go forth instruction,
>> and the word of the Lord from Jerusalem.
> He shall judge between many peoples,
>> and shall arbitrate between strong nations far away;
> they shall beat their swords into plowshares,
>> and their spears into pruning hooks;
> nation shall not lift up sword against nation,
>> neither shall they learn war any more;
> but they shall all sit under their own vines and under their
>> own fig trees,
>> and no one shall make them afraid;
>> for the mouth of the Lord of Hosts has spoken.
>> (Micah 4:1–4)

The message of the Hebrew prophets is profound yet simple: God's *shalom* brings the promise of a universal peace that is based on justice and the renunciation of bloodshed. Jesus' teaching on peace was deeply rooted in the Hebrew prophetic tradition.

Pacifism in the Christian Scriptures

Our understanding of pacifism in Christian history begins with the life, teaching, and death of Jesus of Nazareth. Comparatively little is known about the personal life of Jesus, yet a good deal is known about his public ministry and particularly his death. A brief discussion of his death will help us to understand Jesus' views on peace.

While it is evident that Jesus was very popular with the Jewish people, his enemies included the elitist chief priests and scribes who were threatened by his popularity and what they viewed as his messianic pretensions. The chief priests and scribes conspired against Jesus to have him killed by the Romans. Because they knew that a charge of "blasphemy" would not be considered by the Romans, the chief priests and scribes sought to have Jesus executed for crimes that were political, indeed revolutionary, in nature. They approached the Roman authorities and said: "We found this man perverting our nation, forbidding us to pay taxes to the emperor, and saying that he himself is the Messiah, a king" (Luke 23:2).

These charges would have deeply alarmed the Romans. The charges linked Jesus with the hated Sicarri and Zealot parties whom the Romans regarded as terrorists. These groups were largely revolutionary bands that sought to reestablish a "Jewish" political and religious kingdom that was free of external (Roman) and internal (corrupt religious) oppressors. Since Jesus, like the Sicarri and Zealots, spoke of the "reign" of God, and counseled non-cooperation with Roman authorities, it is understandable that the Romans could have thought Jesus was a revolutionary. Jesus was killed as a Zealot (with two other Zealots or "thieves"), for whom crucifixion was the appropriate form of capital punishment. The reason for Jesus' death was spelled out in the sign nailed to the cross by the Romans, "Jesus of Nazareth, King of the Jews."

Although the biblical authors are rather kind to Pontius Pilate, the historical record tells us that Pilate was a ruthless tyrant. It was, after all, Pilate whose "verdict" resulted in Jesus' crucifixion. When they killed Jesus, the Romans did not waste their time crucifying a harmless ascetic. Jesus was killed as a social revolutionary, in large part because his vision of the "kingdom of heaven" clearly stood in contrast to the violent and exploitative policies of the Roman Empire. When God's rule or kingdom became manifest on earth, there would be no place for empires such as that of Rome that were based on power and greed.

Since the revolutionary parties advocated violence, and since Jesus was identified with these parties, especially in his death, was Jesus in fact an advocate of violence? As we have seen, Jesus shared with the revolutionaries the conviction that the kingdom of God must become manifest in history. But the Sicarri and the Zealots advocated violence as the means to achieve the kingdom. It was here that Jesus departed from them in a significant way. Not only did Jesus have a different understanding of the "kingdom of God," but—more significantly—he renounced the "eye for an eye" ethic of retaliation. For Jesus, a peaceful kingdom had to be founded on justice and nonviolence.

In his very first public appearance at his home town in Galilee (a hotbed of revolutionary activity), it was clear that Jesus stood in the prophetic tradition of grounding the kingdom in justice. The following passage was foundational for his entire ministry and served as the remote context for his death:

> When he came to Nazareth, where he had been brought up, he went to the synagogue on the sabbath day, as was his custom. He stood up to read, and the scroll of the prophet Isaiah was given to him. He unrolled the scroll and found the place where it was written:
> "The Spirit of the Lord is upon me,
> because he has anointed me
> to bring good news to the poor.
> He has sent me to proclaim release to the captives
> and recovery of sight to the blind,
> to let the oppressed go free,
> to proclaim the year of the Lord's favor." (Luke 4:16–19)

The "poor," the "captives," the "blind," and the "oppressed" were, of course, those Jews who were the victims of the Roman policy of taxation and military subjugation, and of the rich Jewish landlords who treated the peasants unjustly. The "political" or "earthly" dimension of God's kingdom appears in many of Jesus' parables and sermons.

Further, by quoting Isaiah, Jesus clearly is rooted in the Jewish prophetic tradition that scorned political phoniness and hypocrisy.

The Sermon on the Mount is the "blueprint" of the reign of God that Jesus seeks to establish on earth. This is the "good news" that Jesus preached to the masses and that infuriated the rich and powerful of his day. In the several verses before the sermon, we gain some understanding of the popularity of Jesus:

> Jesus went throughout Galilee, teaching in their synagogues and proclaiming the good news of the kingdom and curing every disease and every sickness among the people. So his fame spread throughout all Syria, and they brought to him all the sick, those who were afflicted with various diseases and pains, demoniacs, epileptics, and paralytics, and he cured them. And great crowds followed him from Galilee, the Decapolis, Jerusalem, Judea, and from beyond the Jordan. (Matthew 4:23–25)

Jesus then begins the sermon with the recitation of the beatitudes:

> When Jesus saw the crowds, he went up the mountain; and after he sat down, his disciples came to him. Then he began to speak, and taught them, saying:
> "Blessed are the poor is spirit, for theirs is the kindgom of heaven.
> "Blessed are those who mourn, for they will be comforted.
> "Blessed are the meek, for they will inherit the earth.
> "Blessed are those who hunger and thirst for righteousness, for they will be filled.
> "Blessed are the merciful, for they will receive mercy.
> "Blessed are the pure in heart, for they will see God.
> "Blessed are the peacemakers, for they will be called children of God.
> "Blessed are those who are persecuted for righteousness' sake, for theirs is the kingdom of heaven.
> "Blessed are you when people revile you and persecute you and utter all kinds of evil against you falsely on my account. Rejoice and be glad, for your reward is great in heaven,

for in the same way they persecuted the prophets who were before you." (Matthew 5:1–12)

These words resonate very strongly with the prophetic vision of Mary, the mother of Jesus, who stated in the *Magnificat*: "He has brought down the powerful from their thrones, and lifted up the lowly; he has filled the hungry with good things, and sent the rich away empty" (Luke 1:52–53).

The reconciliation of enemies is a central mandate of the Sermon on the Mount. After telling his listeners that they should not even be "angry" with or "insult" a brother or sister, Jesus states:

> "So when you are offering your gift at the altar, if you remember that your brother or sister has something against you, leave your gift there before the altar and go; first be reconciled with your brother or sister, and then come and offer your gift." (Matthew 5:23–24)

Rather than counseling hatred, revenge, or violence against a neighbor who "has something against you," Jesus counsels his followers to forgive and to worship with hearts that are free of hatred and filled with love.

Turn the Other Cheek

Perhaps there is no more famous passage that has been used to defame or ridicule pacifism as the "turn the other cheek" section of the Sermon on the Mount. This passage is popularly interpreted as counseling "passivism" or inaction in the face of insult and injustice:

> "You have heard that it was said 'An eye for and eye and a tooth for a tooth.' But I say to you, Do not resist an evildoer. But if anyone strikes you on the right cheek, turn the other also; and if anyone wants to sue you and take your coat, give your cloak as well; and if anyone forces you to go one mile, go also the second mile. Give to everyone who begs from you, and do not refuse anyone who wants to borrow from you." (Matthew 5:38–42)

Jesus then goes on to further explain his counsel not to "resist an evildoer":

> "You have heard that it was said, 'You shall love your neigh-
> bor and hate your enemy.' But I say to you, Love your ene-
> mies and pray for those who persecute you, so that you may
> be children of your Father in heaven; for he makes his sun
> rise on the evil and on the good, and sends rain on the right-
> eous and on the unrighteous. For if you love those who love
> you, what reward do you have? Do not even the tax collec-
> tors do the same? And if you greet only your brothers and
> sisters, what more are you doing than others? Do not even
> the Gentiles do the same? Be perfect therefore, as your heav-
> enly Father is perfect." (Matthew 5:43–48)

There are three observations that are appropriate concerning these passages.

The first observation deals with the counsel, "do not resist." Some scholars and Christian pacifist sects have interpreted this counsel literally and have held that Christians must be passive in the face of attacks on their person, their families, or their nation. Another interpretation, however, is that the counsel of non-resistance could well read: "Do not resist as the Zealots do," or "Do not resist using violence," or "Do not use violence, but by all means resist." We must remember that Jesus was mistaken as a Zealot (because of his support of the kingdom), but it is quite clear that, unlike the Zealots, he neither preached hatred nor raised an army to resist the hated Romans. Recent research, however, suggests that Jesus *did in fact* counsel resistance in the Sermon on the Mount, as we shall see in what follows.

The second observation concerns the counsels to "turn the other [cheek]," to "give your cloak as well," and to "go also the second mile." Were these really passive counsels that advocated the humiliation of Jewish people in the face of Roman occupation and institutionalized injustice? According to scholar Walter Wink in his critically acclaimed *Engaging the Powers* (1992), these were not counsels of passivity but rather counsels of nonviolent resistance. Wink makes the following points:

1. The counsel to "turn the other [cheek]" concerns a master/servant relationship:

Why then does he counsel these already humiliated people to turn the other cheek? Because this action robs the oppressor of the power to humiliate. The person who turns the other cheek is saying, in effect, "Try again. Your first blow failed to achieve its intended effect. I deny you the power to humiliate me. I am a human being just like you. Your status does not alter that fact. You cannot demean me." (176)

2. The counsel to "give your cloak" concerns the creditor/debtor relationship:

Why then does Jesus counsel them to give over their undergarments as well? This would mean stripping off all their clothing and marching out of court stark naked! Imagine the guffaws this saying must have evoked. There stands the creditor, covered with shame, the poor debtor's outer garment in the one hand, his undergarment in the other. The tables have suddenly been turned on the creditor. The debtor had no hope of winning the case; the law was entirely in the creditor's favor. But the poor man has transcended this attempt to humiliate him. He has risen above shame. At the same time, he has registered a stunning protest against the system that created his debt. He has said in effect, "You want my robe? Here, take everything! Now you've got all that I have except my body. Is that what you'll take next?" (178–179)

3. The counsel to "go also the second mile" concerns the soldier/subject relationship between the Romans and the Jews (occupation troops could compel subjects to carry their pack for one mile, but no more):

Imagine the soldier's surprise when, at the next mile marker, he reluctantly reaches to assume his pack, and the civilian says, "Oh no, let me carry it another mile." Why would he want to do that? What is he up to? Normally, soldiers have to coerce people to carry their packs, but this Jew does so cheerfully, and will not stop! ... From a situation of servile impressment, the oppressed have suddenly seized the initiative. They have taken back the power of choice. The soldier is thrown off balance by being deprived of the predictability of his victim's response. (182)

Professor Wink concludes his analysis of these forms of "nonviolent direct action" with the insight that, "To those whose lifelong pattern has been to cringe before their masters, Jesus offers a way to liberate themselves from servile actions and a servile mentality" (p. 183).

The third observation concerns the command to "Love your enemies and pray for those who persecute you" or, in Luke's words, "Love your enemies, do good to those who hate you" (Luke 6:27). Prayer is, in this context, the spiritual act of wishing God's *shalom* on one's persecutors and enemies. When those who persecute others live according to God's peace, they will *stop* their persecution, *repent* for their sins, and seek *reconciliation* with those they have harmed. Doing "good" to those who hated the Jews meant using nonviolent force to prevent them from doing greater evil. Love is always an active force that seeks liberation, justice, and happiness for others, especially one's enemies.

The gospels record that Jesus' commitment to nonviolence extended even to his death. We can imagine that if there ever was a time when Jesus would urge his followers to use violence against his enemies, it would have occurred just hours before his death when Jesus was betrayed by his disciple Judas. After Judas identified Jesus with a kiss, Jesus was arrested by a crowd of soldiers and police. What followed was a violent response in defense of Jesus:

> Suddenly, one of those with Jesus put his hand on his sword, drew it, and struck the slave of the high priest, cutting off his ear. Then Jesus said to him, "Put your sword back into its place; for all who take the sword will perish by the sword." (Matthew 26:51–52)

Jesus was then led to the Jewish high priests. They in turn sent him to the Romans, who were responsible for his execution as "King of the Jews."

Hence, some Christian pacifists believe that active resistance to evil, the work of social justice, and the reconciliation of enemies are the cornerstones of the Christian peacemaker. The Sermon on the

Mount is not some abstract pie-in-the-sky formula for the afterlife: it is a call to a revolution of the heart that will empower people to take control of their lives and the social structures that dominate them. The Sermon on the Mount provides both a "vision" and a "blueprint" for a new social order that is based on justice and love.

The Armor of God

The early Christians believed that Jesus' death on the cross created a radically different social order, one that was based on justice and reconciliation. St. Paul writes eloquently in his epistles of the new world order that was created by "redemption through [Jesus'] blood." In Paul's letter to the Ephesians, he contrasts the Christian "soldier" with the Roman soldier of his day:

> Finally, be strong in the Lord and in the strength of his power. Put on the whole armor of God, so that you may be able to stand against the wiles of the devil. For our struggle is not against enemies of blood and flesh, but against the rulers, against the authorities, against the cosmic powers of this present darkness, against the spiritual forces of evil in the heavenly places. Therefore take up the whole armor of God, so that you may be able to withstand on that evil day, and having done everything, to stand firm. Stand therefore, and fasten the belt of truth around your waist, and put on the breastplate of righteousness. As shoes for your feet put on whatever will make you ready to proclaim the gospel of peace. With all of these, take the shield of faith, with which you will be able to quench all the flaming arrows of the evil one. Take the helmet of salvation, and the sword of the Spirit, which is the word of God. (Ephesians 6:10–17)

This passage helps us to understand that the true enemies of the Christian are not the Romans or any external force; the enemies of the Christian are the demonic forces within. Paul states that the Christian struggle is not against "enemies of blood and flesh," but rather against "the cosmic powers of this present darkness." The only effective defense against these spiritual enemies is found in "truth," "righteousness," "peace," "faith," and "salvation," which alone can defeat these "spiritual forces." For the Christian, the armor of earthly armies is useless in resisting evil; only the "armor of God" will suffice.

Pacifists, then, believe that the mission of Jesus was to establish the reign of God's peace *(shalom)* on earth and throughout the universe. Jesus accomplished this through active love of his enemies expressed in the form of nonviolent resistance. Pacifists note that Jesus could have, along with other revolutionaries of his time, engaged in violence and hatred of the enemies of the Jewish people, but he did not. Instead, he offered himself as an innocent victim whose death redeemed all people from their sins. The crucifix is the symbol of the redemptive nature of self-suffering.

Among the last words of Jesus to his disciples we read, "Peace I leave with you; my peace I give to you" (John 14:27). The peace of Jesus was, however, to be defined differently by his followers in the two millennia that followed: some followers were pacifists, some engaged in limited war, some fought brutal Crusades, and some sought World Community. Ironically, all did so for peace, sincerely believing that the path they had chosen would lead to the abolition of war and eternal salvation.

The following perspectives on pacifism can be found in the Hebrew and Christian Scriptures:

- Peace *(shalom)* is God's gift to a just society.
- Universal peace is possible on earth.
- Peace is the liberation of those who are physically and
    spiritually poor.
- Spiritual—not physical—weapons are required to make
    peace on earth.
- Reconciliation of enemies is central to a Christian vision
    of peace.
- Love of enemies requires nonviolent resistance to evil.

The Pacifism of the Early Christians

For the first several centuries following Jesus' death, pacifism was the dominant Christian witness. While there are isolated examples of Christians who served in the Roman military after 170 CE,

Christians almost universally shunned military service—and other forms of violence—well into the fourth century. Why were these early Christians pacifists?

There are four reasons offered to explain the pacifism of the early Christians:

1. *Repudiation of idolatry* (the worship of false gods). The early Christians refused to acknowledge the divinity of Caesar because their allegiance was exclusively to the reign of God. Since Roman soldiers (especially the officer corps) had to worship Caesar, it is understandable that Christians would not have wanted to serve in the Roman military.

2. *The imminent eschato*n (second coming of Christ). There is certainly evidence in the Christian Scriptures that the followers of Jesus thought the reign of God to be imminent. Since the end of the world was about to happen, why then care about the affairs of the world? The expectation of an impending eschaton did not, however, last beyond the first century.

3. *An aversion to Rome.* Rome often brutally persecuted the early Christians as an unpatriotic religious sect. It follows that Christians, therefore, would be unlikely to participate in their own persecution. It is worth noting, however, that this reason applied only at certain times and in certain regions of the Roman Empire; there were emperors who did not persecute the Christians and, when there were persecutions, they took place only in select areas of the empire.

4. *Love of enemies.* The earliest Christians refused to serve in armies because they rejected the "eye for an eye" ethic and accepted Jesus' command to love their enemies. For these Christians, participation in war and military service were incompatible with the gospel of reconciliation.

While each of these reasons has some bearing on the pacifism of the early Christians, the fourth is the strongest, since it existed well into the fourth century and could be found throughout the Roman Empire. Support for war and military service is rarely expressed by

Christian writers of this period. On the contrary, there is abundant evidence that the early Christians were forbidden to serve in the military because they were already "soldiers of Christ." Let us look at some of the pacifist texts from early Christianity:

The *Didache* (composed between 70 and 90 CE). "Bless those who curse you, and pray for your enemies, and fast for those who persecute you. For what reward is there for loving those who love you? Do not the Gentiles do the same? But love those who hate you, and you shall not have an enemy." (I)

Justin Martyr (100–165 CE). "We who were filled with war and mutual slaughter and all wickedness have each and all throughout the earth changed our instruments of war, our swords into ploughshares and our spears into farming-tools, and cultivate piety, justice, love of humankind, faith and the hope which we have from the Father through the Crucified One." (*The Dialogue with Trypho*, 110)

Tertullian (160–220 CE). "The Lord, in disarming Peter, ungirt every soldier." (*On Idolatry*, 19)

Origen (185–254 CE). "To those who ask us where we have come from or who is our commander, we say that we have come in accordance with the counsels of Jesus to cut down our warlike and arrogant swords of dispute into ploughshares, and we convert into sickles the spears we formerly used in fighting. For we no longer take sword against a nation, nor do we learn any more to make war, having become sons of peace for the sake of Jesus, who is our commander." (*Against Celsus*, 5, 33)

Maximilian (274–295 CE). "I will never serve you. You can cut off my head but I will not be a soldier of this world, for I am a soldier of Christ.... I will not take the badge [of the soldier]. If you insist, I will deface it. I am a Christian, and am not allowed to wear that leaden seal around my neck. (*Acts of Maximilian*)

Martin of Tours (316–397 CE). "Hitherto I have served you as a soldier, let me now serve Christic.... I am a soldier of Christ and it is not lawful for me to fight."

Canons of Hippolytus (third to fifth centuries CE). "Of the magistrate and the soldier: let them not kill anyone, even if they receive the order to do so; let them not put crowns on. Anyone who has an authority [as a judge or soldier] and does not do the justice of the gospel, let him be cut off and not pray with the bishop. Let...a believer...if he desire to be a soldier, either cease from his intention or, if not, let him be rejected." (Canon 13)

Pelagius (ca. 350–ca. 420 CE). "He is a Christian who does not know how to hate even his enemies but rather to do good to his adversaries and pray for his persecutors and enemies, following Christ's example; for anyone who is ready to hurt and harm someone else lies when he declares that he is a Christian. The Christian is one who is able to make the following claim with justification: I have harmed no man, I have lived righteously with all." (*On The Christian Life*, 6, 1)

The early Christian attitude toward war and military service was pacifism. Christians either refused to participate in armed forces or resigned from the military if they were converted while soldiers. Some soldier-converts were executed for their pacifism. Rather than kill their enemies, the early Christians sought to convert their enemies through the power of love. They insisted that the only effective way to overcome enemies was through performing good works for these very enemies. According to historian Roland Bainton (1960): "All varieties of early Christian pacifism had in common an emphasis on love and an aversion to killing."

Although there is no evidence of Christians serving in the Roman army prior to 170 CE, there is evidence that some Christians were soldiers after that. But, as the above quotation from the *Canons of Hippolytus* illustrates, Christians who served as soldiers could no longer do so if they were ordered to shed blood. How then could they be soldiers at all? They could be soldiers because Roman soldiers also served as police and diplomats and these forms of service were not rejected by Christians. After a thorough study on Christians and the military, Jean-Michel Hornus in his book *It Is Not Lawful for Me to Fight* (1980) concludes that the "basic disciplinary law of the primitive Church" that was in force from the first years of the third century into the fifth century included these stipulations:

1. Anyone who is either a Christian or a catechumen is absolutely forbidden to join the army.

2. Anyone who was a soldier at the time of his conversion and who is an ordinary ranker may if necessary remain one, but only on condition that he neither becomes involved in warfare nor becomes guilty of homicide.

3. For anyone who occupies a position of responsibility, such tolerance cannot be maintained. Such a person must give up his Christian position if he wishes to become a Christian. (167, 168)

Conscientious objection to military service—both *before* enlistment and *after* enlistment—has a long history that can be traced back to the witness of the early Christians.

To sum up, the following perspectives on pacifism may be found among the early Christians:

- Jesus' command to love enemies required reconciliation of enemies.
- Military service that involved bloodshed was forbidden for Christians.
- Followers of Christ were to pray for and to do good to those who persecuted them.

Clerical Pacifism

A subtle but substantive change in the Christian attitude toward war took place in 313 CE when the Edict of Milan, promulgated by the Roman emperor Constantine, recognized Christianity as a legitimate religion of the empire. Prior to the Synod of Arles in 314 CE, Christians had been *forbidden* to serve in the Roman army, but by 416 CE *only* Christians were permitted to serve as soldiers. By this time Christianity was the "official" religion of the Roman Empire. Gradually, over time and with the theological justification of Ambrose and Augustine, Christians were permitted to kill—shed blood—in warfare. Why? The answer to this question will be discussed in the next chapters that deal with the just war model and the Crusades.

Before moving on to that discussion, however, we should note that while pacifism ceased to be the dominant position of Christians on warfare after the fourth century, pacifism has continued to exist through the centuries into our own time.

In the fourth and fifth centuries, as Neoplatonic thought (which holds that the human spirit is dragged down by the human body) took hold, and as the Roman political order *(Pax Romana)* became the vehicle for the spread of the Christian church *(Pax Christiana),* pacifism moved from a social to a personal realm, with monks and clergy serving as pacifism's chief witnesses. Pacifism was required of women and men who entered monasteries or convents, and the secular clergy (those who lived in society) were also exempt from shedding blood in war.

Monastic and mendicant communities founded by Anthony of Egypt and Augustine in the fourth century, by Benedict and Scholastica, and Columba in the sixth century, and by Francis of Assisi and Clare in the thirteenth century all expected their members to live in harmony and peace. The Rule of St. Benedict is representative when it requires monks "to love one's enemies; not to curse them that curse us, but rather to bless them; to bear persecution for justice sake" (Rule of St. Benedict, IV).

In the thirteenth century, scholastic theologian Thomas Aquinas (1225–1274) in his monumental *Summa Theologica* offered two reasons why clergy and bishops are not permitted to shed blood. The first reason is that "warlike pursuits are full of unrest, so that they hinder the mind very much from the contemplation of Divine things, the praise of God, and prayers for the people which belong to the duties of a cleric." The second reason connects clerical pacifism to the Eucharist:

> The second reason is a special one, because, to wit, all the clerical Orders are directed to the ministry of the altar, on which the Passion of Christ is represented sacramentally, according to 1 Cor. Xi. 26: *As often as you shall eat this bread, and drink the chalice, you show the death of the Lord, until He comes.* Wherefore it is unbecoming for them to slay or shed blood, and it is more fitting that they should be ready to shed their own blood for Christ, so as to imitate in deed what

they portray in their ministry. (*Summa Theologica,* II-II, Q.40, Art. 2)

In addition to clerics not being permitted to engage in warfare, they were also forbidden to participate in capital punishment or to command mercenary troops. The Fourth Lateran Council (1215) stated:

> No cleric may decree or pronounce a sentence involving the shedding of blood, or carry out a punishment involving the same, or be present when such punishment is carried out. ...Moreover no cleric may be put in command of mercenaries or crossbowmen or such like men of blood. (18)

It is ironic that these rules against clerical participation in war and killing were issued during the period of the church-sponsored Crusades (holy wars) against the "Saracens" or followers of Islam. (We will discuss the Crusades in the chapter on total war.) The fact that laypeople may kill in warfare and clerics may not is a moral dilemma that continues to our own time. This dual standard exists even in the military: Christian chaplains may *not* take up arms, while Christian soldiers *must* take up arms. Pacifists contend that this is an example of Christian inconsistency and hypocrisy. "Why should the rules be any different for laypeople than for clerics?" they contend. "Is not everyone baptized into the same faith? Do not all share in God's love for all people, including enemies?" In some Christian denominations, the gap between moral expectations relating to clergy and those relating to laypeople continues to this day.

Medieval Pacifism

Except in monastic and clerical communities, pacifism became almost extinct as a social witness within Christianity during the early medieval period. In 800 Charlemagne was crowned Holy Roman Emperor and the church became the effective ruler of much of Europe. By the year 1000 war had become common among Christian princes and Christian knights were venerated for their prowess in battle and at tournaments. The Catholic Church sometimes enthusiastically accepted warfare and soldier-saints became venerated.

In the medieval period, practices crept into the church that caused it to lose the gospel vision that called for simplicity of life and gentleness of spirit. Clergy sought worldly riches and political power in order to support lavish lifestyles. The church became a major landowner and exploiter of the poor in Europe and even some of the great cathedrals that were erected during this period were built with slave labor. Church officials sold indulgences to finance construction projects in Rome. Church offices were bought and sold. Some bishops and popes even owned—and fought in—armies. The church was in need of reform.

During the first half of the eleventh century, the church sponsored two sets of laws designed to severely limit warfare between Christians. The Peace of God exempted monks, clergy, women, merchants, shepherds, pilgrims, peasants, and even sheep and olive trees from warfare. The Truce of God exempted Sundays, Fridays, holy days, and whole church seasons (such as Advent) from warfare. These laws were not, however, strictly pacifist in nature, since the church continued to accept warfare, albeit of a very limited variety. In addition, there is evidence to suggest that a major purpose of the Peace of God and especially the Truce of God was to produce harmony at home so the church could be unified in the forthcoming (1095) holy war against Islam. Nevertheless, the Peace of God and the Truce of God influenced the growing body of international law that exempted civilians from war and that called for a truce to be observed during certain times of the year. (In the chapter on the just war model we will have more to say about the Peace of God and the Truce of God as formal attempts to set limits on war.)

The pacifist ideal again appeared in the late twelfth century with the advent of a pacifist sect known as the Waldensians. This was a group of lay preachers who stressed the call to poverty and the authority of the Bible on moral issues. Although they were condemned by the Catholic Church in 1215, their influence continued into the Reformation.

Franciscan Pacifism

In the thirteenth century, Francis of Assisi (ca. 1182–1226), a former soldier and prisoner of war, founded the Franciscans, a mendicant order dedicated to voluntary poverty and personal pacifism. The Franciscan movement significantly contributed to the lessening of wars between Italian city states by granting laypeople Franciscan protection as members of a "Third Order" (Tertiaries) who were exempt from military conscription. Concerning lay Franciscans, the Rule of the Third Order (1221) stated, "They are not to take up lethal weapons, or bear them about, against anybody."

The Franciscan Tertiaries, along with other groups including the Disciplinati and the Bianchi, gave rise to the thirteenth-century peace movement known as the "Great Alleluia." This peace movement was widely popular and demonstrates that pacifism existed even during the period of total war known as the Crusades. Indeed, there was widespread opposition to these "holy" wars, especially from the laity. The Franciscan Third Order also provided a medieval example of the fact that Catholics may be conscientious objectors to war.

The Franciscan movement did not, however, advocate pacifism for the leaders of the Catholic Church. Francis himself accompanied the Fifth Crusade and, although he personally tried to convert the Islamic sultan (he failed), he did not condemn the Crusade itself. Apparently, Francis thought he would be martyred in his attempt to convert the sultan. Francis's polite reception by the sultan, therefore, was unexpected.

The English Franciscan and scientist Roger Bacon (1214–1294), however, did condemn the Crusades as counterproductive to converting the Saracens, contending that "the faith did not enter the world by arms but by simple preaching." Roger Bacon, joined by the Dominicans William of Tripoli and Raymond of Pennafort, lamented that people "persist in their error" because "the truth is not preached to them in their own language." The movement known as "missionary pacifists" was to foreshadow the great sixteenth- and seventeenth-century missionary efforts of the Society of Jesus (Jesuits), who knew and respected the cultures and religions of those they sought to convert.

A few Franciscans even participated in the military. In the fifteenth century, for example, the Franciscan John of Capistrano (1385–1456) led a church-sanctioned Crusade against the Turks. Nevertheless, down to our own time the Franciscans and many other religious orders have maintained the personal witness of pacifism in a Catholic Church that has been either at war itself or often justifying war for others.

In 1415 a Czech priest, Jan Hus, was executed by Catholic officials for attacking clerical abuses and supporting scriptural authority over the authority of the church. Hus's witness inspired a follower, Petr Chelcicky, to found the pacifist Czech Brethren, who renounced war as unchristian and condemned the state for waging war. This group, like some others, was to abandon its strict pacifism in the centuries that followed.

Humanist Pacifism

By the sixteenth century it was not uncommon for popes, bishops, priests, and even monks to engage in warfare. The Renaissance humanists, staunch critics of a church that had forgotten its scriptural and patristic roots, called upon the church to return to its pacifist heritage. Prominent among the humanists were John Colet (1467–1519) and Thomas More (1478–1535) of England, Juan Luis Vives (1492–1540) of Spain, Guillaume Bude (1467–1540) of France, and Desiderius Erasmus (ca. 1466–1536) of The Netherlands. John Colet was representative when he stated, "It is not by war that war is conquered, but by peace, and forbearance, and reliance on God."

The most famous of the Renaissance humanists on peace issues, however, was Erasmus of Rotterdam. Writing in *Praise of Folly* (1509) Erasmus lamented the fact that the church that had been founded on the blood of nonviolent martyrs had now made "it legal for a man to draw his sword, kill his brother with it, and still be considered to be of the greatest charity—charity which, according to Christ, is due every man by his neighbor." Erasmus's strongest condemnation of the hypocrisy of church leaders is found in his most pacifist work, *Complaint of Peace* (1517). Erasmus states,

What do miters and helmets have in common? What has a crosier to do with a sword? What has a Bible to do with a shield? How can one reconcile a salutation of peace with an exhortation to war; peace in one's mouth and war in one's deeds? Do you praise war with the same mouth that you preach peace and Christ? Do you herald with the same trumpet both God and Satan?...What filth is the tongue of a priest who exhorts war, evil, and murder!"

It is said of Erasmus that "he laid the egg and Luther hatched it." Although Erasmus never left the Catholic Church, his works were placed on the Catholic Church's "Index of Forbidden Books" in 1559 and ordered to be burned.

Centuries of protests inspired by pacifist-oriented theologians and activists like Erasmus in Holland, Jan Hus in Bohemia, and John Wyclif (ca. 1328–1384) in England would culminate in the Reformation that was initiated when Martin Luther (1483–1546) attached his famed ninety-five theses to a church door in Wittenberg, Germany in 1517. Luther attacked many church abuses, including the selling of indulgences and clerical corruption.

Luther did not, however, in any serious way challenge the church's teaching on war. Luther, an Augustinian monk, continued to hold to just war principles. He refused to support the Peasants' War of 1524–1525, *not* because he was opposed to war itself, but rather because the peasants lacked sufficient authority to wage war. Indeed, wars of religion were to follow in the wake of the Reformation in which Protestant Christians enthusiastically killed Catholic Christians, Catholic Christians slaughtered Protestant Christians, and both groups executed Christian pacifists.

The Historic Peace Churches

The sixteenth-century Reformation gave rise to three Christian churches that were dedicated to the nonviolent witness of the Sermon on the Mount as the cornerstone of the Christian attitude toward war: the Anabaptists (sixteenth century), the Society of Friends, or Quakers (seventeenth century), and the Brethren (eighteenth century). They are known as the "historic peace churches." These churches—while at times differing on their relationship to the secular order—have maintained a pacifist witness since their foundation. Subject to violent suppression and political exclusion by both Protestants and Catholics, the peace churches have consistently refused to legitimize war as a Christian enterprise. A brief word about each.

Anabaptists. In the early sixteenth century, Conrad Grebel (ca. 1498–1526) and his associates, believing that the reforms begun in Zurich, Switzerland, by Huldrych Zwingli had not gone far enough in restoring the spirit of the early Christians to the church, began to put into practice radical teachings. These included rejection of infant baptism, re-baptism of adults (hence "Anabaptist"), nonconformity to the world, the rejection of oaths, the practice of humility, simplicity, a communitarian way of life, and pacifism. In Grebel's words, "True Christians use neither the worldly sword nor war, for among them killing has been totally abolished."

Major branches of the Anabaptists that have survived to our own time are the Hutterites, founded by Jacob Hutter (d. 1536), and the Mennonites, inspired by Menno Simons (d. 1561). In the United States, the Old Order Amish are perhaps the most well known Mennonite community. Related pacifist groups include the Schwenckfelders and Moravians. A contemporary example of the Anabaptist tradition is the Bruderhof Communities, which are dedicated to "nonviolence, simplicity, and service."

Society of Friends (Quakers). The English cobbler George Fox (1624–1691) believed that there was within each person a God-given "inner light" that pointed the path to salvation. This teaching rejected the doctrine of the innate depravity of humankind and, in effect, made every Christian a priest who could be directly inspired by the Holy Spirit. Fox preached a radical Christian doctrine that was centered on pacifism. When asked, for example, why he would not become a soldier, he replied, "I live in the virtue of that life and power that takes away the occasion of all wars." From the beginning, he and his associates were headed for trouble with civil authority. Fox and others were jailed in England and hanged in the American colonies (Mary Dyer is a notable example) for their convictions.

In about 1650 Fox and his associates formed what was to become the Religious Society of Friends (popularly known as the "Quakers"). In 1660 the Friends stated, "We utterly deny all outward wars and strife, and fightings with outward weapons, for any end, or under any pretense whatever; this is our testimony to the whole world." From their inception the Friends have maintained a constant witness that values the equality of women and men, supports charitable projects to help those in need, and seeks civil legislation to promote social justice and respect for the sanctity of conscience.

In addition to their opposition to war, the Friends are regarded as a preeminent major force behind the abolition of slavery, the securing of voting rights (suffrage) for women, efforts to abolish war, and numerous other social causes. Indeed, throughout their history, the Friends have exerted a degree of influence on civil matters far greater than their numbers would lead one to expect.

Brethren. The Church of the Brethren began in Germany in 1708 when a small band of women and men under the leadership of Alexander Mack formed an adult covenant to follow the teachings of Jesus Christ as found in the Christian Scriptures. "Conviction, covenant, compassion, and conversation" have characterized Brethren communities and their approach to the civil order. Rather than focusing on a doctrinal creed, the Brethren concentrate on ethical teachings that have a foundation in the gospels: pacifism, temperance, a refusal to take oaths, and simplicity of life. The peace witness of the Brethren, like that of the Anabaptists and Friends, has often resulted in their being persecuted and imprisoned.

Though always small in number, the historic peace churches have been large in spirit and have given strong witness to nation states that the higher law of conscience must dominate civilized societies. Members of these churches have been socially ostracized, jailed, tortured, and killed for their pacifism and they serve as a reminder that courage is not the exclusive province of the soldier. Today's nation states presume that young men and women are willing to kill other young men and women for their flag. It is this presumption that the peace churches call into question. Because of that, they are considered to be either unpatriotic or dangerous to the nation state. The historic peace churches are living testimony to the observation in 1897 of the Russian Petr Verigin, "The most dangerous element in Christianity, from the point of view of the established order, is the refusal to kill a human being."

The peace churches were not alone in their pacifist stance. More mainstream Christian churches, including the Methodists, Baptists, Anglicans, Presbyterians, Congregationalists, and Unitarians, also had strong pacifist tendencies and many supported conscientious objection to war. In addition, these churches often linked their pacifism to related issues such as the abolition of slavery and the right of women to vote.

Salient aspects of pacifism in medieval and Reform Christian history include the following:

- Pacifism was still required of monks and clergy after laity were allowed to participate in war.
- The Peace of God and the Truce of God were laws designed to limit wars between Christians.
- The Franciscan Tertiary movement exempted laypeople from military conscription.
- Christian humanists denounced as hypocrites clergy who waged war.
- The historic peace churches called Christians to their early Christian pacifist roots.

Nineteenth- and Twentieth-Century Peace Witness

The nineteenth century saw the rise of non-sectarian or secular societies that subscribed to pacifism, whether of the "principled" or "pragmatic" variety. These included the London Peace Society (1815), the New England Non-Resistance Society (1838), and the International Peace Bureau (1892). A leading voice for peace in Europe was Austrian Bertha von Suttner (1843–1914) whose anti-war novel *Lay Down Your Arms* turned many from war to peace. Baroness von Suttner's labors for peace through arbitration resulted in the Hague Conferences of 1899 and 1907 that gave rise to the World Court. She also influenced Alfred Nobel (the inventor of dynamite) to found the Peace Prize.

Perhaps the most famous Christian spokesperson for peace in the nineteenth century was the author of *War and Peace*, Leo Tolstoy (1828–1910). Tolstoy explained the basis for his pacifism in his books, *What I Believe* and *The Kingdom of God Is within You.* He believed that the teachings of Jesus required Christians not to swear and to love their enemies. Consequently, he renounced institutions that relied on violence: governments, courts, armies, police, and private property. Tolstoy influenced many to form agricultural communes and his views on nonviolence had a strong impact on Mohandas K. Gandhi and the Catholic Worker movement.

The twentieth century gave rise to numerous peace organizations, many of which have consultative status at the United Nations. We can discuss only a few of these organizations (more information is easily available through Web sites).

Fellowship of Reconciliation (FOR). The FOR was founded in 1914 by Henry Hodgkin, a British Quaker, and Friedrich Siegmund-Schultze, a German chaplain who vowed to stand for peace in what was to become the Great War (1914–1918). Since that time, the movement has become international and its activities include opposition to war; the struggle for economic and racial justice; support for conscientious objectors; participation in civil, environmental, and feminist rights movements; and prison reform and abolition of the death penalty. This broad spectrum of activities is rooted in the FOR's conviction that opposition to war "must be based on a commitment to the achieving of a just and peaceful world community, with full dignity and freedom for every human being" (Statement of Purpose, FOR/USA).

The American section of the FOR includes the following peace fellowships: Baptist Peace Fellowship, Brethren Peace Fellowship, Buddhist Peace Fellowship, Catholic Peace Fellowship, Church of God Peace Fellowship, Disciples Peace Fellowship, Episcopal Peace Fellowship, Jewish Peace Fellowship, Lutheran Peace Fellowship, Methodist Peace Fellowship, Muslim Peace Fellowship, Presbyterian Peace Fellowship, Unitarian-Universalist Peace Fellowship. The International Fellowship of Reconciliation (IFOR), headquartered in The Netherlands, has chapters and affiliates in Africa, Asia, Europe, Latin America, North America, and Oceania. Dr. Martin Luther King Jr. was one of the more notable members of the FOR.

American Friends Service Committee (AFSC). The AFSC is a Quaker organization that was founded in 1917 to assist Quaker and other conscientious objectors to serve the victims of World War I in France, Germany, and Russia. Through the years this Nobel Peace Prize winning organization (1957) has assisted poor people in Appalachia, relocated Jewish refugees from Nazi Germany, participated in the civil rights movement, assisted draft resisters during Vietnam, strongly supported the Nuclear Freeze Campaign, sought to end non-military sanctions against Iraq, and called for justice, not retaliation, in response to 9/11.

The numerous justice and peace activities of the AFSC are based on its conviction that "there is that of God in each person." Because the AFSC asserts "the transforming power of love and nonviolence as a challenge to injustice and violence and as a force for reconciliation" the group regards "no person as our enemy." As it has in every war since their foundation, the AFSC continues to counsel and support people in forming their conscience on matters of war and peace.

War Resisters League (WRL). Although it is not a faith-based or Christian organization, the pacifist War Resisters League (WRL) deserves a word here. Founded in 1923, the WRL's Statement of Purpose reads, "The War Resister's League affirms that all war is a crime against humanity. We therefore are determined not to support any kind of war, international or civil, and to strive nonviolently for the removal of all causes of war." The WRL has defended the rights of conscientious objectors and has been active in the anti-war and civil rights movements. It also advocates civil disobedience to unjust laws and war tax resistance.

The Catholic Worker Movement. The Catholic Worker was founded in New York City in 1933 by Peter Maurin (1877–1949) and Dorothy Day (1897–1980). This lay movement stresses the works of mercy, voluntary poverty, pacifism, war resistance, opposition to racism, and simplicity of life. The movement sponsors almost two hundred independent "houses of hospitality" that provide volunteers the opportunity to express their faith through prayer and action. Many "Workers," including Dorothy Day, have been jailed for their conviction that war must be resisted through civil disobedience to unjust laws. A central mission of the movement is the publication of the *Catholic Worker,* a newspaper that explains the "Christian personalist" philosophy of the Catholic Worker and offers commentary on day-to-day affairs at Worker houses along with commentary on world events.

The movement has been most prominently associated with Dorothy Day, who converted to Catholicism in 1927 after having championed socialist causes through a career in journalism. The movement was severely tested during World War II when—much to the dismay of many supporters—Dorothy Day wrote: "We continue our pacifist stand." Stating that "our manifesto is the Sermon on the Mount," Dorothy Day and her Catholic Worker sisters and brothers have maintained a consistent pacifist Catholic witness from World War II to the wars in Iraq. Dorothy Day and the Catholic Worker movement contributed mightily to the reawakening of pacifism in the Roman Catholic tradition.

Catholic Peace Fellowship (CPF). Because pacifism for laypeople had practically disappeared from official Catholic teaching since the fifth century, Catholic applications for conscientious objector status as late as World War II were strongly resisted by the state. It was widely assumed that Catholics must support war rather than peace. The pacifist Catholic Peace Fellowship was founded in 1965 by Jim Forest and Tom Cornell to demonstrate that a Catholic could be a pacifist and that, in fact, there was a long tradition of pacifism in Catholic history. Gradually, largely due to CPF's influence, it became much easier for Catholics to receive CO status.

The CPF provides materials for Catholics—civilians and military—who are considering application for CO status to the draft; it engages in educational activities that promote peacemaking in the Catholic Church; it opposes ROTC at Catholic universities and high schools; and it provides information for military chaplains concerning regulations for those who apply for CO status while in the military.

Pax Christi International (PCI). Although it is not strictly a pacifist organization, the lay Roman Catholic movement Pax Christi deserves to be discussed in this chapter because of its very strong pacifist orientation and the exclusively nonviolent strategies and programs that it advocates. Pax Christi was founded in France in 1945 by a group of lay Catholics led by Martha Dortel-Claudot. The group received the support of Bishop Pierre Marie Theas, who had been a prisoner under the Nazis, and its immediate focus was reconciliation between French and German Catholics. Pax Christi, known also as the "International Catholic Movement for Peace," became intercontinental in the early 1970s when chapters were established in Australia and the United States. Today Pax Christi has member chapters and affiliates in more than thirty countries on five continents and enjoys consultative status at the United Nations.

From its foundation Pax Christi has been an organization that has worked for reconciliation, disarmament, human rights (including conscientious objection), peace education, the spirituality of nonviolence, and a just world order. These, and many related activities, are achieved through Pax Christi International's five goals: solidarity, dialogue, training, advocacy, and networking. Pax Christi USA was founded in 1972 and it immediately set about to make "peacemaking" a priority for the Catholic Church in the United States. In one of its important contributions to peacemaking, Pax Christi USA formulated the "Vow of Nonviolence." Pax Christi members take, or renew, this vow at their annual assemblies. Here is the text:

A VOW OF NONVIOLENCE

Recognizing the violence in my own heart, yet trusting in the goodness and mercy of God, I vow to practice the nonviolence of Jesus who taught us in the Sermon on the Mount:

Blessed are the peacemakers, for they shall be called sons and daughters of God.... You have learned how it was said, "You must love your neighbor and hate your enemy"; but I say to you, "Love your enemies and pray for those who persecute you. In this way, you will be sons and daughters of your Father in heaven."

Before God the Creator and Sanctifying Spirit, I vow to carry out in my life the love and example of Jesus by striving for peace within myself and seeking to be a peacemaker in my daily life; by accepting suffering rather than inflicting it; by refusing to retaliate in the face of provocation and violence; by persevering in nonviolence of tongue and heart; by living conscientiously and simply so that I do not deprive others of the means to live; by actively resisting evil and working nonviolently to abolish war and the causes of war from my own heart and from the face of the earth.

God, I trust in your sustaining love and believe that just as you gave me the grace and desire to offer this, so you will also bestow abundant grace to fulfill it.

John Dear explains this vow in some detail in *Disarming the Heart: Toward a Vow of Nonviolence* (1987).

Liberation through Non-Violence

During the civil rights struggles in mid-twentieth-century America, Dr. Martin Luther King Jr. inspired a large number of black and white women and men to embrace nonviolence. In *Why We Can't Wait* (1963) Dr. King describes the nonviolent army:

We did not hesitate to call our movement an army. But it was a special army, with no supplies but its sincerity, no uniform but its determination, no arsenal except its faith, no currency but its conscience. It was an army that would move but not maul. It was an army that would sing but not slay. It was an army that would flank but not falter. It was an army to storm bastions of hatred, to lay siege to the fortresses of segregation, to surround symbols of discrimination. It was an army whose allegiance was to God and whose strategy and intelligence were the eloquently simple dictates of conscience.

Dr. King believed that nonviolence would save the "soul" not only of the nation but of the Christian church as well. He spoke for many when he stated:

But the judgment of God is upon the church as never before. If today's church does not recapture the sacrificial spirit of the early church, it will lose its authenticity, forfeit the loyalty of millions, and be dismissed as an irrelevant social club with no meaning for the twentieth century.

Dr. King's challenge to the church in the twenty-first century remains the same.

Church Statements on Pacifism

In the United States today, most pacifists of draft age (generally 18–26) apply for the status of conscientious objector (CO) to military service in the event of a mandatory military draft. A mere letter informing the government of the petitioner's personal convictions against war, however, will not be accepted by the government. A CO must substantiate his or her "claim" to that status by (1) appearing before her or his local draft board, (2) providing written documentation that describes "how he arrived at his beliefs; and the influence his beliefs have had on how he lives his life"; and (3) providing evidence from others (written and/or in person) that support the CO claim. (This information is taken from the official United States Selective Service System Web site: www.sss.gov.)

An acceptable source for documenting "how" a person arrived at her or his convictions and for describing the "influence" the beliefs have had on a person's life is the official teaching on war and peace of the church to which that person belongs. The Center on Conscience and War (formerly the National Interreligious Service Board for Conscientious Objectors, or NISBCO) has—since 1951—published *Words of Conscience: Religious Statements on Conscientious Objection* as an aid to persons making a CO claim. *Words of Conscience* includes statements from humanist, Baha'i, Buddhist, Christian, Jewish, and Unitarian Universalist religious bodies.

The following diverse Christian religious bodies have statements on war and conscience that can be found in *Words of Conscience*: Assemblies of God–General Council; Association of Bible Students; American Baptist Churches–USA; Church of the Brethren; Church of Christ, Scientist; Church of God (Seventh Day); Community of Christ; Episcopal Church; Religious Society of Friends (Quakers); Greek Orthodox; Jehovah's Witnesses; American Lutheran Church; Mennonite Central Committee; United Methodist Church; National Council of Churches of Christ in the U.S.A.; United Presbyterian Church; Roman Catholic Church; Salvation Army; Seventh Day Adventists; Sojourners; United Church of Christ; and the World Council of Churches.

Very few of these Christian religious bodies are exclusively pacifist churches. Each, however, supports pacifism as a form of personal witness for its members. Some do so by recalling that pacifism is the oldest and most authentic Christian witness, while others accept pacifism an one of several responses—including military service—that a Christian may make to war.

The Roman Catholic Church recognizes a diversity of positions concerning participation in war. As such, it is representative of the vast majority of Christian churches in their teaching on war and conscience. The biblical, theological, and historical support the Catholic Church offers for both pacifism and military service is typical of many Christian churches. The following quotations are from contemporary documents that recognize the right to pacifism for Catholics.

From the Second Vatican Council (1963–1965):

For this reason, all Christians are urgently summoned "to practice the truth in love" (Eph. 4.15) and to join with all true peacemakers in pleading for peace and bringing it about. Motivated by this same spirit, we cannot fail to praise those who renounce the use of violence in the vindication of their rights and who resort to methods of defense which are otherwise available to weaker parties too, provided that this can be done without injury to the rights and duties of others or of the community itself.... Moreover, it seems right that laws make humane provisions for the case of those who for reasons of conscience refuse to bear arms, provided, however, that they accept some other form of service to the human community. (*Gaudium et Spes:* Pastoral Constitution on the Church in the Modern World, 1965, 78–79)

From the American Catholic Bishops:

In light of the Gospel and from an analysis of the Church's teaching on conscience, it is clear that a Catholic can be a conscientious objector to war "because of religious training and belief."... As we hold individuals in high esteem who conscientiously serve in the armed forces, so also we should regard conscientious and selective conscientious objection as positive indicators within the Church of a sound moral awareness and respect for human life. (United States Catholic

Conference "Declaration on Conscientious Objection and Selective Conscientious Objection," 1971)

One must ask, in light of recent history, whether nonviolence should be restricted to personal commitments or whether it should also have a place in the public order with the tradition of justified and limited war. National leaders bear a moral obligation to see that nonviolent alternatives are seriously considered for dealing with conflicts. New styles of preventative diplomacy and conflict resolution ought to be explored, tried, improved and supported. As a nation we should promote research, education and training in nonviolent means of resisting evil. Nonviolent strategies need greater attention in international affairs. (United States Catholic Conference, "The Harvest of Justice is Sown in Peace," 1993)

These official statements of the Catholic Church reflect positions taken by many Christian churches on issues of war and peace. While mainstream Christian bodies have long promulgated the just war model as their official teaching, the return in the late twentieth century to pacifism as a legitimate Christian witness is perhaps the most notable feature of contemporary Christian teaching on war and peace.

This return may cause some people to fear, and others to welcome, the prospect that the twenty-first century will witness mainstream Christian churches joining the historic peace churches in renouncing bloodshed and advocating pacifism as *the* authentic Christian witness with regard to war.

Terrorism and Pacifism

The terrorist events of September 11, 2001, that killed close to three thousand people posed a serious challenge not only to pacifism but to traditional military doctrine as well. "Why did this happen?" "Why us?" "How should we respond?" were some of the questions that Americans asked themselves immediately after that fateful day.

Some people demanded immediate retaliation and even nuclear destruction of Islamic states whether they were involved in 9/11 or not (total war). Others held out for a measured military response that would target the group or nation that had sponsored the attacks (just war). Some people advocated "doing good" to the offending party by changing the unjust policies that had caused the attack or by sending massive amounts of human and material assistance to those who had attacked the United States (pacifism). Another group called for the matter to be brought to the World Court and the International Criminal Court to secure changes in international law that would permit an international police force to arrest the offending parties (World Community). The responses ranged from retaliation to reconciliation.

Before examining the pacifist response to terrorism, however, a word needs to be said about the "end" and "means" of terrorism.

Terrorism is a political strategy that seeks a radical policy change on the part of the entity or nation that is attacked. While the "end" or goal of terrorism is sometimes revenge or punishment, terrorism more frequently seeks to change specific practices (abortion or environmental destruction, for example), or to change public or international policy in order to secure social justice or political or religious freedom (Basque independence, or Palestinian statehood). Although terrorism is popularly associated with non-state actors (such as the IRA or Al-Qaeda), nation states also employ terrorist tactics to secure political ends (death squads or obliteration bombing).

The "means" that terrorists employ attempt to produce policy changes on the part of the offending party through the use of fear instilled by unacceptable loss of civilian life or property damage. Consequently, terrorists use strategies that kill or injure innocent persons in large numbers. They believe that the greatest loss of innocent life will produce the greatest policy change on the part of the offending party. Some terrorists accept the fact that terrorist acts may initially achieve little in the way of results. Consequently, terrorists believe that repeated acts of terrorism over a long period of time will produce their desired ends.

A pacifist response to terrorism would endorse:

- ***Nonviolent intervention.*** Because of the extensive number of nonviolent NGOs (non-governmental organizations) in many countries, pacifists can easily predict future trouble spots in the world. Terrorism can be prevented through early intervention by such organizations as Peace Brigades International (PBI), the Nonviolent Peace Force (NPV), international centers for dispute resolution, and international aid programs, as well as through preventive diplomacy by nation states. The United Nations has enjoyed a great deal of success in preventing or limiting conflicts through its Economic and Social Council, the International Court of Justice, and the famed "Blue Berets." Religious bodies can abandon support for war and promote reconciliation between warring parties.

- *Peaceful means to peaceful ends.* Inspired by Jesus and Gandhi, pacifists believe that "we reap exactly as we sow" and "permanent good can never be the outcome of untruth and violence." The pacifist view is that terrorism is doomed to fail because hatred and violence will create only greater animosity and bloodshed rather than peace and harmony. No mind was ever changed through hatred and no heart was ever converted through violence. If those who were offended by U.S. policies had used nonviolent resistance instead of airplanes targeted at innocent people, their resistance would have converted the American people to their cause, just as many Romans were converted by the nonviolence of the early Christians, or the English people were converted by the nonviolent tactics of Gandhi in India.

- *The Golden Rule.* Pacifists believe that "doing unto others as we would have them do unto us" is an extremely effective guide for personal and political behavior. Hence, if we would be bombed and attacked, then we should first do it to others; on the other hand, if we would be loved and respected, then we must treat others with love and respect. The terrorists responsible for the 9/11 attacks on the United States had done "unto the United States" what the United States "had done unto others." The U.S. responded with massive bombing and military attacks that have injured and killed thousands of innocent people in two countries.

- *Peace through justice.* Pacifists follow the biblical insight that justice alone is the secure foundation for peace. Police forces and soldiers can maintain or even restore order, but peace can come about only when people are treated in accordance with their dignity as human persons and creatures of God. Terrorism often is the result of unjust social policies that must be changed if terrorist activity is to cease. What poor countries need is not occupation troops or torture, but clean water, medical care, employment, and education. Some pacifists responded to 9/11 with the call, "Send in the Peace Corps."

Many pacifists believe in police forces and the coercive power of domestic and international law. But they think it is immoral and counterproductive to use violence as a method to secure justice. In their view, "we reap as we sow."

Conclusion

Pacifism, whether in the form of non-resistance or nonviolent resistance, has existed since humans have fought wars. It exists in almost every culture that has been studied and it is at the heart of many religions. Even those religions that endorse a militant response to "outsiders" require pacific behavior among their own adherents. In fact, some leaders urge their citizens to support war abroad in order to secure peace at home.

Christianity began as a pacifist religion and pacifism was the dominant witness during the first several centuries of its existence. As time went on, pacifism was abandoned as the dominant model, first with the shift to the just war in the fifth century and later in the shift to the total war model in the eleventh century during the Crusades. Still, pacifism has always existed as a personal witness throughout Christian history. For much of that history, pacifism has been required of those who anticipate the reign of God on earth—monks, friars, and the clergy. In addition, there have always been "reform" movements within Christian history that have called for a return to the primacy of the Christian Scriptures and to that time when all

Christians—laypeople as well as clergy—were called to witness to the reign of God on earth.

In the early twenty-first century numerous churches have endorsed pacifism as official Christian teaching, even though many continue to accept participation in war for defensive purposes and as a last resort. Hence, for example, one Catholic may in good conscience be a conscientious objector to military service while another Catholic, also in good conscience, may fight in a just war.

Nevertheless, pacifism remains the oldest Christian response to war.

The Pacifist Model: A Summary

These are key points that characterize the pacifist model:

1. Human beings are naturally peaceful. The desire for survival, and for the security that guarantees survival, indicates that peace is the normal end or goal of humankind. Cooperation, harmony, and love express the essence of human nature and are found universally in human communities. Conflict is natural and healthy for humans; when resolved in a creative fashion, it provides justice for all parties to a dispute.

2. Social justice is the foundation of peace. Authentic peace can exist only in societies that guarantee such rights and necessities as safe drinking water, a living wage, fair prices, affordable housing, medical care, education, legal protection, religious tolerance, cultural protection, and political freedom. Societies that survive in peace are secure in justice.

3. Resistance should be nonviolent. Survival and security cannot be achieved without conflict, whether it be on a personal, social, or international level. While persuasion and diplomacy are the ideal ways to resolve conflict, some disputes can be resolved only through forceful actions. We must resist injustice, but we must do so by using nonviolence weapons. Nonviolent resistance employs force or power to secure justice without hating or injuring an opponent.

4. We must love our enemies. Love is a positive force that seeks to restore and heal an enemy's injured humanity. Love means performing good works on another's behalf, even though such acts may be unwelcome or rejected. Love requires patience, kindness, and courage to stay the course until an enemy acts justly or restores injured rights. Love turns enemies into opponents, and opponents into friends.

5. Means and ends are instrinsically linked. Authentic peace can be achieved only through peaceful means, never through violence such as war. As Gandhi taught, "means and ends" must ever be convertible terms: just as peace cannot produce war, so war cannot produce peace. In the words of A. J. Muste, "There is no way to peace; peace is the way."

6. There are no "good" guys and no "bad" guys. Some human actions may be understood as "good" or "evil," but pacifists contend that there is in every evil person some good, just as there is in every good person some evil. Human beings are on a pilgrimage to full humanity, and at times individuals and governments take mistaken paths out of malice, ignorance, or immaturity. Humility requires that we first admit our own mistakes before seeking to correct those of another. Understanding the evil in another's heart begins with an examination of one's own heart.

7. Civilians should be trained in nonviolence. There is a long history of unarmed citizens who have used nonviolence to resist injustice at home or to prevent invasion from abroad. Every citizen should be trained in the use of nonviolent "weapons" to resist attack and to convert one's enemies. A highly trained and motivated nonviolent civilian defense force or nonviolent international intervention force that includes every citizen can be effective in deterring and, if necessary, conquering enemies.

8. Schools must educate for courage. The purpose of far too many schools is to educate for obedience and conformity. Education for courage teaches people to secure accurate facts, to think critically about them, and to put their convictions into action. Courage means being able to accept—without retaliation—cultural rejection, and even jail and death, for that which one holds to be true or sacred. Courage is the cardinal virtue of the pacifist.

9. Reconciliation is the goal. While conflict management and conflict resolution are important goals for the peacemaker, none is more important than the reconciliation of enemies. To unite warring parties into sisters and brothers who share together, work together, and celebrate together is the supreme mission of the peacemaker. A joyous heart and a willing spirit can accomplish the seemingly impossible: the unity of all.

10. There is hope for the future. Despite the sad record of violence and war, human beings have survived—and thrive—because love is stronger than hate and cooperation is more effective than competition. Courageous individuals and determined social movements can secure a world free of want and full of peace. A world community founded on universal human rights and secured by law can turn prophetic visions into reality. The finest pages of human history have yet to be written.

———————— • ————————

At the end of the first chapter of this book, you were asked to write a letter to Nicole expressing your own views on war. Now that you have completed this chapter on pacifism, write her another letter, this time answering the following questions:

1. What is the biblical basis for pacifism?

2. Why was the early Christian church pacifist?

3. What are the three most important historical stages in the development of pacifism?

4. How does pacifism respond to terrorism?

5. What, in your opinion, are the three most important key points of the pacifist model?

You can finish your letter by stating your own view on pacifism. You might discuss what you consider to be its strong points and weak points.

This information will be very helpful to Nicole as she struggles with the moral problem of war. But neither she nor you will be able take an intelligent stand on war until you consider the information contained in the next three chapters. We turn now to a discussion of the just war model.

Recommended Reading

The following books are recommended if you would like to learn more about pacifism:

Dale W. Brown. *Biblical Pacifism.* 2nd ed. Herald Press and Evangel Publishing House, 2003.
Eileen Egan. *Peace Be with You: Justified Warfare or the Way of Nonviolence.* Orbis Books, 1999.
John Ferguson. *The Politics of Love: The New Testament and Non-Violent Revolution.* James Clarke Publishers, 1970.
Jean-Michel Hornus. *It Is Not Lawful for Me to Fight.* Herald Press, 1980.
Ronald G. Musto. *The Catholic Peace Tradition.* Orbis Books, 1986; reprint ed. Peace Books, 2002.
Walter Wink. *Engaging the Powers: Discernment and Resistance in a World of Domination.* Fortress Press, 1992.

Just War

"The love of enemies admits of no dispensation,
but does not exclude wars of mercy
waged by the good."
Augustine of Hippo

Introduction

War is a political institution that employs lethal methods to re-solve conflict between states.

Wars exist at the *inter*national level (between nation states) or at the *intra*national level (civil wars). Although lethal conflict takes place between religions, tribes, gangs, and even families, the use of the word "war" normally refers to disputes between nation states or alliances. Wars are fought for territorial and economic gain; to settle cultural, philosophical, or religious differences; to defend against at-tack; to defend the innocent in another nation; to establish empire; or to carry out revenge and retaliation.

As William Eckhardt observes in *Civilizations, Empires, and Wars* (1992), generally three conditions are necessary for a success-ful war: (1) a *surplus population* of young people to fight the war, (2) *surplus wealth* to finance the war, and (3) the *moral support* of a nation's citizens. Hence, while surplus or expendable population and wealth are necessary, they are not in themselves sufficient conditions for waging a successful war.

An effective war can be waged only with the will and support of the people. When a nation's population withdraws its moral support for a war, the cause may be lost no matter how wealthy a nation is, or how large or effective its fighting forces are, or, for that matter, how expert its military leadership is. Hence, moral support and popular justification are foundational to the successful prosecution of any war.

Although peace is the stated goal of all participants in war, each side nevertheless contends that it alone stands on the side of justice. Consequently, most wars become conflicts between "good" and "evil" and the destruction of the "evil" party is essential for the establishment or restoration of peace. This "good guy" versus "bad guy" philosophy tends toward the indiscriminate destruction of the opposing party.

There is, therefore, a very heavy moral burden placed on civilian leaders and military officers who would lead young men and women into war and who would ask a nation's people to support a war. How do leaders know if they are on the side of "justice" in a given dispute or if they are truly fighting for "peace"? How can they in fact tell the "good guys" from the "bad guys" in war? Who is right and who is wrong? And is there a way of limiting the indiscriminate nature of war?

Throughout history, just war principles (referred to by some as the just war "theory") have been a major source of ethical guidance in war. These principles seek to: (1) *curtail* the right to go to war (*"ius ad bellum"*—the right to go to war), (2) *limit* the damage that is done in conducting a war (*"ius in bello"*—conduct in war), and (3) *repair* the damage caused by war (*"ius post bellum"*—justice after war or "just termination").

There is in the just war model a *moral presumption against war*. War, for example, must be fought strictly as a "last resort"; killing in war is restricted to those who actually participate in military operations; and the good that results from the war must outweigh the evil inflicted by the war. These principles for "limited" war (we will examine "total" war in the next chapter) are found wherever war is fought and they are the basis for many international treaties.

The just war model was developed over many centuries, as we shall see in the following pages. For ease of reference, we provide here a listing of the just war principles that are generally accepted today:

I. Right to Go to War (Ius ad Bellum)

1. *Just cause.* A war must be fought in defense of "innocent" human life or to protect violated rights.
2. *Proper authority.* A nation's legally constituted authority must declare war. International law should be respected.
3. *Right intention.* The intention in going to war must be to restore peace. Revenge is forbidden.
4. *Last resort.* All peaceful alternatives must be exhausted before war is declared.

II. Conduct in War (Ius in Bello)

5. *Probability of success.* A war must be winnable.
6. *Just conduct.* Only active military combatants are legitimate targets in war. Civilians may not be killed.
7. *Proportionality.* The good to be achieved must outweigh the evil that is done in war.

III. Justice after War (Ius post Bellum)

8. *Just Termination.* A "conditional"—rather than "unconditional"—surrender should be negotiated.
9. *Restitution.* A victor in war has a moral obligation to repair damage done during the war to innocent people and the nation's infrastructure.

Although war as a human social institution is comparatively new in human history (war began with the "territoriality" of agricultural societies about ten thousand years ago), the practice of seeking to limit its destruction is as old as war itself. Some variation of the just war principles can be found in preliterate and aboriginal societies and in the ancient and classical cultures of Africa, Asia, Europe, and what became the Americas. We turn now to a discussion of the just war model in Christian history.

Just War in the Hebrew Scriptures

As we saw in the last chapter, a strong foundation for Christian pacifism can be found in the Hebrew Scriptures. Nevertheless, while nonviolence as a path to peace is an important dimension of Jewish ethical behavior, the Jews also fought wars to extend their territory or to provide for their security. A relatively few of these wars were offensive or "total" wars; these will be discussed in the next chapter. Some wars the Jews fought were of a defensive or "limited" nature and logically fall into the category of just war. We should note, however, that for much of Jewish history even defensive war was not an option for Jews because of constant persecution, especially by Christians.

Since Jewish ethical behavior is strongly influenced by the Ten Commandments, people are sometimes confused by the commandment "You shall not kill" (see Exodus 20:13; Deuteronomy 5:17). "Doesn't this forbid *all* killing?" they ask. The answer is no. Scholars tell us that this commandment should properly read "You shall not murder" (and it is in fact translated this way in the New Revised Standard Version). Hence, killing in war, and capital punishment, were allowed under Jewish ethical law. Murder was not permitted because it involved the taking of "innocent" life, while war and capital punishment were permitted because they took the lives of people who were "guilty" of crimes of transgression. Therefore, the commandment not to "kill" meant that Jewish people could not kill "innocent" people.

In fact, the Hebrew Scriptures record instances in which God *requires* death as a punishment for those who are guilty of certain crimes. Examples include the following:

> But if someone willfully attacks and kills another by treachery, you shall take the killer from my altar for execution. (Exodus 21:14)

> Whoever strikes father or mother shall be put to death. (Exodus 21:15)

> You shall not permit a female sorcerer to live. Whoever lies with an animal shall be put to death. Whoever sacrifices to any god, other than the LORD alone, shall be devoted to destruction." (Exodus 22:18–20)

These examples illustrate two points: (1) that capital punishment is divinely sanctioned in Jewish law, and (2) that in Jewish law there must be sufficient cause in order to inflict capital punishment. (As the centuries have passed, Jewish law has been modified to provide less drastic punishment for certain crimes.)

The attempt in Jewish ethical thought to *limit* the violence that could be used either in punishment or war is called the "Law of Talion." Rooted in the Code of Hammurabi (Babylon, eighteenth century BCE), the Law of Talion is based on just compensation for a crime that was either (1) actually committed, or (2) unjustly alleged to have been committed. There are many versions of the Law of Talion in the Hebrew Scriptures, but perhaps the most famous are the "eye for an eye" passages. We read,

> If any harm follows, then you shall give life for life, eye for eye, tooth for tooth, hand for hand, foot for foot, burn for burn, wound for wound, stripe for stripe. (Exodus 21:23–25)

> Anyone who kills a human being shall be put to death. Anyone who kills an animal shall make restitution for it, life for life. Anyone who maims another shall suffer the same injury in return, fracture for fracture, eye for eye, tooth for tooth; the injury inflicted in the injury to be suffered. (Leviticus 24:17–20)

The concept of "retaliation" or "revenge" is often associated with the Law of Talion, giving it a far more negative meaning than was originally intended. Retaliation connotes a punishment that is *greater* than the offense, as in taking two eyes, for example, for one eye. People who advocate revenge similarly seek to exact compensation that is *greater* than the crime itself as in, for example, requiring a thief to pay five times the money he or she originally stole. The Law of Talion is a legal measure that severely *limits* retaliation and revenge. It promotes justice between hostile parties by letting "the punishment fit the crime."

The Jews applied the "limitation" that is found in the Law of Talion to the conduct of war. The following passage is illustrative:

> When you draw near to a town to fight against it, offer it terms of peace. If it accepts your terms of peace and surrenders to you, then all the people in it shall serve you in forced

labor. If it does not submit to you peacefully, but makes war against you, then you shall besiege it; and when the LORD your God gives it into your hand, you shall put all its males to the sword. You may, however, take as your booty the women, the children, livestock, and everything else in the town, all its spoil. You may enjoy the spoil of your enemies, which the LORD your God has given you. (Deuteronomy 20:10–14)

This passage places the following limitations on war: (1) war must be a last resort that may be waged only after pursuing peaceful alternatives to war; and (2) killing in war must distinguish between adult males (soldiers) and women, children, animals, etc. These two limitations—war as a last resort and the prohibition of killing of civilians— are found in the classic just war principles.

The concept of using people and animals as "booty" or "spoils" in war is not found in the just war principles but is more in keeping with the total war model. Nevertheless, the notion that wars have limits and that an ethical code of conduct should regulate wars is clearly found in the Hebrew Scriptures. Other examples of the concept of limited war can be found in 2 Kings 6:20–23 and 2 Chronicles 28:5–15.

Just War in the Christian Scriptures

The Hebrew Scriptures serve as the main source that Christians have used to justify participation in warfare. This is particularly true for the concept of "Crusade" or "total" war that we shall examine in the next chapter. There are, however, several passages in the Christian Scriptures that have been used to justify participation in warfare for Christians. These passages are sometimes called the "warrior" passages. We turn now to a brief discussion of them.

"Give to the emperor the things that are the emperor's..."

Perhaps the most popular passage in the Christian Scriptures that is used to justify military service is the famous "Render unto Caesar" or "Give to the emperor" passage. We read:

> Then they sent to him some Pharisees and some Herodians to trap him in what he said. And they came and said to him, "Teacher, we know that you are sincere, and show deference to no one; for you do not regard people with partiality, but teach the way of God in accordance with truth. Is it lawful to pay taxes to the emperor, or not? Should we pay them, or should we not?" But knowing their hypocrisy, he said to them, "Why are you putting me to the test? Bring me a denarius and let me see it." And they brought one. Then he said to them, "Whose head is this, and whose title?" They answered, "The emperor's." Jesus said to them, "Give to the emperor the things that are the emperor's, and to God the things that are God's." And they were utterly amazed at him. (Mark 12:13–17; see also Matthew 22:15–22 and Luke 20: 20–26)

While this passage does not explicitly mention military service, just war advocates interpret the passage to mean that there is an implicit mandate for patriotism and military service in Jesus' statement, "Give to the emperor the things that are the emperor's...." Clearly, they argue, in this passage Jesus tells his followers to pay tax to and cooperate with the Roman emperor—and through him with every political authority. Christians live in *two* realms: the earthly kingdom of politics and the spiritual realm of God. Because of this, Christians have a *duty* to obey civil law, and if the civil authority declares war, then Christians must serve in the military.

This "dual realm" interpretation was widely accepted in Christian history until the advent of modern historical and biblical scholarship. Some scholars offer an alternative interpretation of the passage, one that questions whether it can be interpreted as implicit support for war on the part of Jesus. These scholars contend that Jesus' political enemies were trying to entrap him with the taxation question so that they could have him killed by the Roman occupation authority. In fact, his enemies *expected* Jesus to counsel disobedience to civil authority on the taxation question.

These scholars hold that in making his enemies produce the Roman coin Jesus exposed their collaboration with the despised occupation forces. Since Jewish loyalty was exclusively to God, no religious Jew would have possessed a coin with the graven image of a "strange god"—Caesar—on it. Also, Jesus' enemies in fact accused him of tax resistance when they sought to have him executed by the Romans. Their charge against him was: "We found this man perverting our nation, forbidding us to pay taxes to the emperor, and saying that he is the Messiah, a king" (Luke 23:2). Consequently, these scholars hold that Jesus did not endorse a "dual realm" theology in this passage, since he expected undivided loyalty to the reign of God in human affairs.

"Making a whip of cords, he drove all of them out of the temple..."

Another passage just war advocates advance to demonstrate that war is accepted in the New Testament is the "cleansing" of the temple of exploitive merchants and bankers by Jesus. We read:

> The Passover of the Jews was near, and Jesus went up to Jerusalem. In the temple he found people selling cattle, sheep, and doves, and the money changers seated at their tables. Making a whip of cords, he drove all of them out of the temple, both the sheep and the cattle. He also poured out the coins of the money changers and overturned their tables. He told those who were selling the doves, "Take these things out of here! Stop making my Father's house a marketplace." (John 2:13–16; see also Matthew 21:12–13; Mark 11:15–18; Luke 19:45–48)

Just war advocates interpret this passage to mean that Jesus used violence in this instance because he made "a whip of cords" with which he expelled people and animals from the temple. Hence, since Jesus used a violent method to secure a peaceful end, war is acceptable to Christians as long as the end is peace. Although there are no other instances of Jesus using a whip (or engaging in any kind of physical violence) in the gospels, just war advocates hold that this single instance validates the use of violence and, by extension, Christian participation in war.

As with the previous passage, some scholars interpret this passage differently. They believe that the "means" employed by Jesus to cleanse the temple were of a nonviolent nature. They observe that, although the "corruption in the temple" story can be found in all four gospels, the "whip of cords" is mentioned only in John. The other gospel writers ignore any mention of a whip because Jesus in fact drove out the merchants and bankers not by physical force but by the force of his personality. He was his own "weapon of the spirit." Consequently, these scholars contend, one cannot conclude that Jesus was endorsing bloodshed even in a righteous cause.

"I have not come to bring peace, but a sword..."

A favorite passage of just war advocates is the one in which Jesus actually states, "I have not come to bring peace, but a sword." We read:

> "Do not think that I have come to bring peace to the earth; I have not come to bring peace, but a sword. For I have come to set a man against his father, and a daughter against her mother, and a daughter-in-law against her mother-in-law; and one's foes will be members of one's own household. Whoever loves father or mother more than me is not worthy of me; and whoever loves son or daughter more than me is not worthy of me; and whoever does not take up the cross and follow me is not worthy of me. Those who find their life will lose it, and those who lose their life for my sake will find it." (Matthew 10:34–39; see also Luke 12:51–53; 14:26–27)

Just war advocates interpret this passage to mean that Jesus was justifying (and even advocating) war when he stated that he had come to bring "a sword" to the world. Jesus clearly understood that his message would result in conflict and that even close members of a family would become mutual foes because of him. Although Jesus does not directly advocate violence here, just war advocates believe that it follows logically from his statement. Why else would Jesus have made specific reference to the "sword"?

Another interpretation of the passage, however, is that the "sword" can be properly understood as a symbol of the "division" that results from faithfulness to God (see also Micah 7:6, Luke 12:51, and Hebrews 4:12). This statement would then demonstrate not that Jesus approved of violence but rather that Jesus understood the consequences of his message. Jesus was a realist. He knew that his teachings on love of enemies and renunciation of wealth were bound to create conflict even in people's own homes.

Also, it is instructive to note that in a similar passage Luke uses the word "division" rather than "sword." We read: "Do you think that I have come to bring peace to the earth? No, I tell you, but rather division" (Luke 12:51). Jesus' acknowledgment of "division" would hardly seem to be an endorsement of bloodshed to resolve the conflicts that are caused by that division.

"And the one who has no sword must sell his cloak and buy one."

In this passage Jesus again makes reference to a "sword" in the context of preaching his message. We read:

> He said to them, "When I sent you out without a purse, bag, or sandals, did you lack anything?" They said, "No, not a thing." He said to them, "But now, the one who has a purse must take it, and likewise a bag. And the one who has no sword must sell his cloak and buy one. For I tell you, this scripture must be fulfilled in me, 'And he was counted among the lawless'; and indeed what is written about me is being fulfilled." They said, "Lord, look, here are two swords." He replied, "It is enough." (Luke 22:35–38)

Just war advocates tell us that this passage must be taken very seriously because just before the beginning of his passion Jesus is telling his followers that they must take up arms in spreading the Christian message. Jesus explicitly tells his disciples to "buy a sword," even if it means selling some of their clothing. A sword was normally carried to defend a person against robbers and enemies (or against animal attack). Military service, therefore, according to just war advocates is mandatory for a Christian in the defense of his or her country.

Some scholars, however, contend that, as in the discussion of the previous passage, the concept of the "sword" acknowledges "division" but it does not mean bloodshed. Jesus was telling his disciples that, like him, they would be viewed by the world as criminals ("counted among the lawless") and they had to be prepared for the "division" their missionary work was sure to cause. Hence, Jesus used the word "sword" in a metaphorical—rather than literal—manner. When the disciples interpret Jesus' words literally and produce two swords ("Look, Lord, here are two swords"), Jesus in essence rebukes them with his response, "It is enough." What he is saying is: "I've had enough of you. You still don't get it. My message is not about bloodshed but about love."

The validity of this interpretation is reinforced by the events that immediately follow. When the temple police come to arrest Jesus in order to put him on trial, a sword is *actually* used by a follower of Jesus. We read:

> When those who were around him saw what was coming, they asked, "Lord, should we strike with the sword?" Then one of them struck the slave of the high priest and cut off his right ear. But Jesus said, "No more of this!" And he touched his ear and healed him. Then Jesus said to the chief priests, the officers of the temple police, and the elders who had come for him, "Have you come out with swords and clubs as if I were a bandit? When I was with you day after day in the temple, you did not lay hands on me. But this is your hour, and the power of darkness!'" (Luke 22:49–53)

It is clear from this passage that Jesus does not endorse the shedding of blood—the literal use of the "sword"—even in the defense of his own life. When an agent of the high priest is attacked by a disciple of Jesus with a sword (some would say justly), Jesus, rather than endorsing this action, heals the servant's ear and states emphatically "No more of this!" Finally, we read in the Gospel of Matthew that Jesus rebukes his follower who used the sword by saying, "Put your sword back into its place; for all who take the sword will perish by the sword" (Matthew 26:52).

Just war advocates believe that the very fact that a follower of Jesus had—and used—a weapon that could draw blood (the sword), and that Jesus' followers at one point produced "two swords," strongly implies that Jesus did not absolutely forbid bloodshed. The fact that Jesus' disciples were carrying weapons at all raises questions about what the gospels *do not* record. Perhaps, as a small group of scholars assert, Jesus was in fact a violent revolutionary (a Zealot) and he did in fact approve of bloodshed.

"A centurion came to him..."

Although we know that Jesus was killed by the Roman military at the command of Roman political officials, there is little evidence that Jesus interacted with the military during the years of his public ministry. Consequently, just war advocates make much of the passage in which Jesus cures the slave of a Roman centurion. (A centurion was a Roman commander of one hundred soldiers.) The passage reads:

> When he entered Capernaum, a centurion came to him, appealing to him and saying, "Lord, my servant is lying at home paralyzed, in terrible distress." And he said to him, "I will come and cure him." The centurion answered, "Lord, I am not worthy to have you come under my roof; but only speak the word, and my servant will be healed. For I also am a man under authority with soldiers under me; and I say to one, 'Go,' and he goes, and to another 'Come,' and he comes, and to my slave, 'Do this,' and the slave does it." When Jesus heard him, he was amazed and said to those who followed him, "Truly I tell you, in no one in Israel have I found such faith." (Matthew 8:5–10; see also Luke 7:1–10)

Just war advocates hold that the very fact that Jesus even speaks with a Roman officer tells us that he was not opposed to the military profession. But Jesus goes further: he praises the faith of the centurion and actually states that it is superior to that of many Jews. For just war advocates, this is clearly proof that, if the military profession is acceptable to Jesus, then it should be to the Christian church as well. Hence, soldiers—especially those who have faith in Jesus— have a special role to play in establishing God's reign on earth.

Some believe, however, that Jesus was praising only the "faith" of the Roman soldier, *not* his profession. The fact that Jesus talks to the centurion and agrees to heal his servant is testimony to the inclusive nature of Jesus' ministry, which excludes no one. It is hardly likely, they argue, that Jesus would be endorsing the profession of soldiers—especially of Roman soldiers, since they were the occupation troops who were usurping God's reign over Israel.

"No one has greater love than this, to lay down one's life for one's friends."

This passage is often used at funerals of soldiers who have died in war. It appears on many war memorials. Just war advocates use it to indicate divine approval not only of *how* the soldier died, but also of *why* she or he died. The soldier died while fulfilling a duty to kill the enemy in order to keep people free. Jesus must, therefore, have endorsed the military profession, since he praises precisely what soldiers are asked to do: die for others.

Biblical commentators point out, however, that this passage must be understood in the context in which it appears. These are among the very last words Jesus speaks to his disciples before he dies at the hands of the Romans, and they are spoken shortly after Jesus has said, "Peace I leave with you; my peace I give to you" (John 14:27). The passage, taken in context, reads,

> "This is my commandment, that you love one another as I have loved you. No one has greater love than this, to lay down one's life for one's friends. You are my friends if you do what I command you. I do not call you servants any longer, because the servant does not know what the master is doing; but I have called you friends, because I have made known to you everything that I have heard from my Father. You did not choose me but I chose you. And I appointed you to go and bear fruit, fruit that will last, so that the Father will give you whatever you ask him in my name. I am giving you these commands so that you may love one another." (John 15:12–17)

How did Jesus love his disciples? Did he personally kill others for his disciples, or lead them into war? As commentators point out, Jesus is referring to his own impending death when he talks about laying down "one's life for one's friends." Jesus died out of love for his friends. Jesus accepted death nonviolently, without advocating hatred for his enemies or retaliation through violence. He died so that people might "love one another." Certainly Jesus did not say, "No one has greater love than to kill for one's friends."

These six passages are the principal texts used by just war advocates to demonstrate that participation in war is acceptable to Christian teaching because it enjoys the support of the gospels. The passages are not unambiguous, since some scholars hold they are either quoted out of context or are used in an isolated "proof text" manner. Nevertheless, they are used to support the proposition that war may be a legitimate Christian enterprise and they have been quoted widely in times of war to justify either war or military service. Related texts used to legitimize Christian participation in war include Matthew 11:12; Mark 13:7–13; John 18:36; Revelation 12:7–9.

In conclusion, even some just war advocates acknowledge that it is only with difficulty that the gospels can be used to justify war as a legitimate Christian endeavor. They correctly assert, however, that there is abundant solid evidence in Christian history that Christian leaders have endorsed war as a Christian enterprise. This evidence dates back to the late fourth century and continues to our own day. We turn now to a discussion of the just war model in Christian history.

From Pacifism to Just War

As we saw in the chapter on pacifism, the early Christians were persecuted and socially ostracized for their faithfulness to the Christian teachings of love of one's enemies and renunciation of wealth. Slowly but surely, however, the nonviolent Christians began to convert the violent Romans. Even enemies said of the Christians, "See how they love one another," and "See how they die for one another." Gradually many Romans, including those who held political power and those who served in the army, converted to Christianity. By the beginning of the fourth century, the Christian religion, while still illegal in the Roman Empire, had expanded to a point at which it could be neither effectively persecuted nor ignored.

In 312 CE the Roman emperor Constantine (ca. 288–337) claimed to have seen a flaming cross in the sky telling him that he would win a battle at the Milvian Bridge (*"In hoc signo vinces"*—"In this sign you will conquer"). After winning this battle, Constantine restored the *Pax Romana* ("Peace of Rome") and in 313 issued the Edict of Milan, which gave Christians the right to freely practice their religion in the empire. This ushered in the period known as the *Pax Christiana* ("Peace of Christ"), and it was during this period that Christians eventually came to accept participation in war.

The gradual change (it took many centuries) from a pacifist church to a church identified with war was the most dramatic shift in Christian ethics in the history of Christianity. How did it happen? Why did it happen? The reasons are varied and include theological, philosophical, and political factors. We turn now to a discussion of three themes or "foundations" upon which the Christian ethic of war was constructed.

1. The Pax Romana *and the* Pax Christiana

With the liberation of Christianity in 313 came the realization on the part of some Christians that the Roman Empire represented the best hope for the spread of Christianity throughout the world. Consequently, some Christian writers held that God had created the Roman Empire so that the Christian faith could be preached everywhere. The *Pax Romana* thus served as the foundation for the *Pax Christiana*.

The fusion between Rome and Christianity had political consequences. Since Christians now enjoyed the protection of the empire and considered themselves citizens of the empire, it was merely a matter of time before their responsibilities as citizens would include military service. The fusion between Rome and Christianity grew so strong that by 380 CE Christianity had become the official religion of the Roman Empire. Within a few decades, *only* Christians could serve as soldiers. Rome's wars had become Christian wars.

2. From Semitic to Platonic Philosophy

Both the Hebrew and Christian Scriptures are founded on a philosophy of human nature that believes the human person is a body/ soul unity. This philosophy is based on a Semitic worldview that sees all that God created as intrinsically good (how could an all-good God create *anything* that was evil?). The Genesis 1 creation story, for example, concludes the six days of creation with the words, "God saw everything that he had made, and indeed, it was very good" (Genesis 1:31). Hence, the entire human person—body and spirit—is naturally good and is born into a world that is "very good."

Platonic thought, on the other hand, posits a radical difference between the human body and the human intellect or soul. Since the soul can achieve perfection only when it is separated from the body, it follows that the body—or material things in general—serve as a hindrance to the "higher" life of the soul. Some Christian thinkers who adopted a Neoplatonic worldview came to despise the body and the material world as threats to salvation.

When this was translated into Christian ethics, normal human bodily activities such as sex, eating, and experiencing any kind of sensual pleasure came to be seen as threats to a person's salvation. Since the human body exists in the "earthly city," human beings are, in the words of Augustine of Hippo (354–430 CE), a "race condemned" to "lawlessness and lust." War, not peace, characterizes the earthly condition of humankind. In fact, killing an enemy in war can even be an act of love, since it liberates the person from the "prison" of her or his body.

3. The Two Kingdoms: Rome and God

At the beginning of the fourth century, Christians were being persecuted by the emperor Diocletian for their alleged lack of patriotism to the Roman Empire. By the beginning of the fifth century, however, Christians enjoyed full Roman citizenship, since Christianity had become the official religion of the empire. Christians now lived in two realms: that of God and that of Rome. As a result, they had obligations to what Augustine of Hippo came to call the "earthly city" and the "city of God."

Some early Christian writers, including Augustine, associated the reign or "kingdom" of God with a spiritual afterlife. There was obviously a vast gulf between "the city of God" and the material "earthly city." The two cities understandably gave rise to two distinct ethical systems. Those "condemned" to live on earth are guided by an ethical system that is based on "fallen" or sinful human nature, while the perfect realization of the Christian life is found only in the spiritual afterlife. (Heaven's ethical system can, however, exist on earth in monastic life and the clerical state, which entail renunciation of material possessions, sexual behavior, and bloodshed.) War, then, is inevitable in the earthly city. Since peace is not possible on earth, wars can be "limited," but they cannot be abolished.

These foundations for just war gradually came together so that by the fifth century CE pacifism was no longer the mainstream wit-

ness of the Christian church. A church now rooted in Roman citizenship adapted to a more pessimistic theology that permitted defense
of the empire as well as of the Christian religion by military means.
We turn now to a discussion of how the theology of the just war developed in Christian history.

Development of the Just War Model: Ambrose and Augustine

The concept of "limited" or just war predates Christian thought.
In the West, the notion of a "just" war is found in the philosophy of
Plato (ca. 428–ca. 347 BCE), Aristotle (384–322 BCE), and Cicero
(106–43 BCE), while in Asia the notion of war as a "last resort" is
found in the philosophy of Confucius (570–490 BCE) and Sun Tzu
(ca. 500 BCE). In fact, a great number of ancient cultures developed
various just war principles.

The Roman philosopher Cicero had a significant impact on the
development of the just war model in Christian theology. Cicero—
writing about war and its limits principally in his treatise *On Duties*
—believed that a war could be just if it was a last resort; if it was
declared by a legitimate authority; if it spared non-combatants; and
if it showed mercy to those who lost the war.

The first thinker to endorse the concept of just war in Christian
history was Ambrose, bishop of Milan (340–397 CE, bishop from
374 to 397). Ambrose, a former lawyer and Roman political official,
advised the emperor Gratian in 378 to pursue "victory over the barbarians" under the protection of the "shields of faith and holding the
sword of the spirit." Writing in *On Duties,* Ambrose demonstrated
the influence of Cicero by telling Christians that "in the matter of
war, care must be taken to see whether the wars are just or unjust."
Ambrose, however, refused to justify violence in personal matters
and also held that priests must refrain from bloodshed because "our
activity has to do not with weapons but with peaceful deeds."

Ambrose formulated his thinking on war during the crucial period in which Christianity became the official religion of Rome (380
CE). His thought on war is distinguished by his association of the
Pax Romana with the *Pax Christiana,* by his view that the courage
of soldiers could be "full of justice," and by his exemption from military service for members of the clergy because "we are concerned

with matters of the soul rather than of the body." The course was now set for the just war model to become the mainstream teaching of the Catholic Church on matters of war and peace.

Ambrose of Milan's contributions to the just war model can be summarized as follows:

- War should defend the weak and oppressed.
- Innocent people may not be killed.
- War must be legally declared.
- Priests and monks may not shed blood.

It was Augustine, bishop of Hippo in North Africa from 395 to 430, however, who became the most famous advocate for just war in Christian history. Augustine studied under, and was baptized by, Ambrose of Milan. Prior to that he had been a member of the Manichean sect, a group that divided the world into competing forces of good and evil, light (spirit) and darkness (matter). By profession, Augustine taught "rhetoric," a field of study that employed persuasive oral and written presentation rather than philosophy in seeking to convert an opponent or win an argument. Augustine's training in rhetoric is reflected in his work.

Although Augustine was later to repudiate Manicheanism, its pessimistic underpinnings nevertheless remained with him and exerted a strong influence on his classic work *City of God*, which divided the world into the "earthly city" and the "heavenly city." The Neoplatonic separation of matter from spirit, of body from soul, of earth from heaven formed the philosophical foundation upon which the Augustinian teaching on war was fashioned.

This philosophical foundation supported Augustine's view that the original sin of Adam and Eve is transmitted biologically from parent to child. In his words, "... from its very start, the race of mortal men has been a race condemned." Accordingly, human beings are born into a state of "innate" depravity due to the "heredity stain" they received from Adam and Eve. In the *City of God*, Augustine taught that the consequences of sin for "the sons of Adam" include "... heartaches, troubles, griefs and fears; such insane joys in discord, strife and war; such wrath and plots of enemies, deceivers, sycophants; such fraud and theft and robbery; such perfidy and pride, envy and ambition, homicide and murder, cruelty and savagery, lawlessness and lust...." Sin, therefore, defines the human condition.

Like his mentor Ambrose, Augustine relied heavily on the philosophy of the non-Christian Cicero for his view on war. Also like Ambrose, Augustine used the Hebrew Scriptures to justify war for Christians. In addition, Augustine formulated his philosophy on war at the very end of the Roman Empire when northern European "barbarians" had already sacked Rome (410 CE) and, in the last years of his life, were attacking Africa. These influences led to Augustine's acceptance of war as a Christian enterprise.

We can better understand Augustine's views on war by briefly considering how he defined peace. Augustine viewed peace as "the tranquility of order" *(tranquilitas ordinis)* or "the calm that comes of order." We read in the *City of God*,

> Peace between a mortal man and his Maker consists in ordered obedience, guided by faith under God's eternal law; peace between a man and a man exists in regulated fellowship. The peace of a home lies in the ordered harmony of authority and obedience between the members of a family living together. The peace of the political community is an ordered harmony of authority and obedience between citizens. The peace of the heavenly City lies in a perfectly ordered and harmonious communion of those who find their joy in God and in one another in God. Peace, in its final sense, is the calm that comes of order. (XIX, 13)

Hence, peace for Augustine is based more on the Roman concept of *pax* (a state of quiet) and the Greek concept of *eirene* (a state of harmony), than on the biblical *shalom* (a state of physical and spiritual integrity).

Because Augustine defines peace as "the calm that comes of order," it is understandable that he would see peace as resting more on "obedience" and "law" than on justice. Hence, it can—and has been—inferred that peace is best pursued through police or military action rather than, for example, human rights and social justice. Although some scholars have rejected this interpretation of Augustine's thought, others have had no difficulty in emphasizing "authority and obedience" as foundational to a "calm" society.

To those who hold that "there can be no peace without justice," some interpreters of Augustine have replied that "there can be nothing without order." Consequently, for them a peaceful society is a place of good order that is grounded in law and protected by police and the military. Later developments—such as totalitarian states (police states) that deny human rights and Catholic Inquisitions (persecutions) that presume guilt before innocence—are sometimes cited as having been influenced by Augustinian views on a peace based on "authority and obedience."

Because Augustine viewed peace as a "state of calm" or quiet, he had a great deal of difficulty with the sometimes conflicting theologies and views of Christian ethics that characterized his time. The Manichean influence that had shaped him led him to see the world in terms of "good" or "evil," "black" or "white" (an exclusionary philosophy that continues to our own time).

Thus, as by far the most influential bishop of his day (or, for that matter, in Christian history), Augustine used imperial (political) power to "compel" differing theologies to conform to the teaching of the Catholic Church. This was particularly true of the Donatists and the Pelagians whom, at times, Augustine called "raging madmen." In varying degrees, Augustine urged "the correction of imperial laws"—suppression, imprisonment, trials, fines, property confiscation, and exile—to compel those with whom he differed theologically to return to their "right minds" and rejoin the Catholic Church.

With regard to imperial edicts, Augustine in his treatise *Correction of the Donatists* stated that "whosoever refuses to obey the laws of the emperors which are enacted on behalf of the truth wins for himself great condemnation." Most important, Augustine held that the recently persecuted Christian church could itself now engage in "a righteous persecution, which the Church of Christ inflicts upon the impious." The Christian church, in short, had an obligation to defend itself against the theological differences that had come to be called "heresies." In historian Peter Brown's words, "Augustine may be the first theorist of the Inquisition."

Augustine taught, however, that the church may persecute only in a "spirit of love" in order to secure the "eternal salvation" of those who were "disturbing the peace of the innocent." Concerning war and love, Augustine stated:

Love does not preclude a benevolent severity, nor that correction which compassion itself dictates. No one indeed is fit
to inflict punishment save the one who has first overcome
hate in his heart. The love of enemies admits of no dispensation, but love does not exclude wars of mercy waged by the
good.

In sharp contrast to the first centuries of Christian history, "war" and
"love" were no longer incompatible terms. The stage was set, then,
for the Catholic Church to participate both in wars of national defense and in wars that defended the church. In almost every "Christian" war that has been fought down to our own time, warring parties
have sought justification from the thought of Augustine of Hippo.

Augustine's contributions to the just war model can be summarized as follows:

- Love of enemies must be the motivation for war.
- War must be declared by the head of state.
- War may be fought to avenge injuries or violated rights.
- The Catholic Church may employ civil authority to combat
  heresy.

The influence of Augustine of Hippo on wars waged by European
powers over the next sixteen hundred years has been monumental.
Augustine's influence lies not so much in the actual "principles" that
he elaborates in a rather unsystematic fashion, but rather in the theology of "fallen man" that undergirds his view of life in the "earthly
city."

It is important to stress, however, that Augustine believed that
war was more a product of sin than of virtue. He condemned "the
desire to do harm, cruel vengeance, a disposition that remains unap-
peased and implacable, a savage spirit of rebellion, a lust for domination and other such things." In fact, Augustine argued that wars
were fought by "good men" to "inflict punishment on things such as
these."

Further, war was to be fought with a "mournful" or "sorrowful"
attitude. Augustine believed soldiers should "grieve" about the
"truly shocking and cruel evils" involved in war. Finally, he advised
that "any one who endures these things [war] or thinks about them

without sorrow in his heart is all the more unfortunate in considering himself happy because, in fact, he no longer possesses any human sensitivity" (emphasis mine). Augustine's purpose was to "limit" war, not to glorify it.

Some theologians hold that Augustine was the first of the great Christian "realists" to recognize the evil that permeates all human social institutions. Others contend that theological "pessimism" and psychological rigidity and intolerance are Augustine's lasting contributions to political discourse. Realist or pessimist, Augustine changed forever the way Christians thought about war. But he neither praised nor glorified war. That was to come later in the Crusades.

The *Penitential Books* on War

By late in the fourth century Christianity was firmly established as the religion of the Roman Empire. Gradually, as the Catholic Church gained political power, and as the Augustinian teaching on just war was integrated into Christian ethics, participation in war became an acceptable vocation for Christians.

During the medieval period (500–1500 CE) that followed the collapse of the Roman Empire, the emphasis on the nature of sin changed. "Personal" or private sins having to do with sexual morality came to be seen as more serious than the "social" sins of idolatry, wealth, and war that had been emphasized in the early church. This was due, in part, to the erroneous assumption that sexual intercourse was the "original sin" committed by Adam and Eve. (In fact, that sin was idolatry.) Also, since a woman had "seduced" a man, it was held that women were more responsible for the evil in the world and should be treated accordingly. Another reason for the decline in emphasis on societal sins was that the Catholic Church wielded a great deal of power over civil society, and organizations in power rarely criticize themselves.

Nevertheless, the church continued to question the morality of war and the conduct of warriors during the early medieval period through the *Penitential Books* and other church "canons" or laws. The *Penitentials* were guides to the sacrament of confession used by Irish missionaries to Europe. These books, designed as aids for uneducated priests (most clergy had little formal education), discussed the nature of sin and the penances to be applied to various types of sins. Common sins in the *Penitentials* included fornication, gluttony, anger, sloth, pride, and homicide. Although the *Penitentials* were not the official teaching of the church, they were widely used and accepted in their time.

The *Penitentials* and other church laws discussed homicide in two ways: as acts committed by individuals (murder) and as acts committed on behalf of the state (war). Homicide was clearly wrong, but what of killing in war? According to the *Penitentials,* soldiers were required to perform acts of penance for killing in war. Such a requirement reflects the influence of the early Christians, who held that war itself was a sinful activity. Thus, even after the concept of the "just" war was accepted by the Catholic Church, killing in war was still considered a crime against God. It is important to note that individual soldiers, not just their commanders, were held accountable for bloodshed. The practice of assigning penance for killing in war existed from the sixth to the twelfth centuries.

The earliest *Penitentials* of Patrick, Finnian, and Columban (sixth century CE) all required penance for clerics and laypeople who either killed in war or committed murder. Other *Penitentials* were explicit in requiring penance for participation in war. They include:

Bigotian Penitential: "He who has killed a man in open war shall do penance for forty days."

The Old Irish Penitential: "Any man who kills a man in battle or in a brawl, or by lying in wait for him [shall do penance] a year and a half or forty nights...."

Penitential of Theodore: "One who slays a man by command of his lord shall keep away from the church for forty days; and one who slays a man in public war shall do penance for forty days."

Fulbert of Chartres, *On Mortal Sins:* "If he kills in a publicly declared war, let him do penance for one year."

Penitential Ordinance **following the Battle of Hastings:** "(1) Anyone who knows that he has killed a man in the great battle, is to do one year of penance for each man killed, according to the number of men killed.... (7) For those who fought in declared war, their bishops, for the sake of mercy, impose three years of penance. (8) Concerning the archers, who kill [at long range] ignorant of their victims, or who wound without homicide, let them do penance for three Lents."

The last point (no. 8) is quite interesting, since it holds morally responsible soldiers who kill at a great distance (for those days!) people they cannot see. Today that principle would apply, for example, to artillery or air forces. It is also quite interesting to note that the individual soldiers (today's enlisted men and women)—not just their civilian or military commanders—were held responsible for killing even soldiers in self-defense. Although peace was the end of war, the means to it—bloodshed—was still widely regarded as a sinful activity.

It is worthy of note that the penances imposed on those who violated the rights of others often required some form of restoration on the part of the perpetrator. The *Penitential of Cummean* is illustrative,

He who by a blow in a quarrel renders a man incapacitated or maimed shall meet [the injured man's] medical expenses and shall make good the damages for the deformity and shall do his work until he is healed and do penance for half a year.

The Law of Talion requiring an "eye for an eye" did not always apply as a form of punishment. Criminals were sometimes subject to a kind of justice known as *restorative justice* or "healing justice" that was practiced by the Celts. A chief purpose of this type of penance was the reconciliation of enemies.

The Peace of God and the Truce of God

Because there were so many independent kingdoms (along with their armies and wars), anarchy reigned in Europe in 1000 CE. People were not safe in their homes or while traveling, and there were no safe times of the week or year to travel. This unsatisfactory situation led to the creation of the Peace of God—laws protecting certain people from attack—and the Truce of God—laws prohibiting violence during certain times of the week or year. The peacemaking activities of the Benedictine monks of this period, particularly those at Cluny, in France, were instrumental in the development of these laws. Both the Peace of God and the Truce of God were introduced in the previous chapter on pacifism, because they were clearly influenced by pacifist philosophy. However, because they set *limits* on war, we will examine them more closely here as aspects of the historical development of the just war model.

As noted in the previous chapter, the Peace of God exempted monks, clergy, women, merchants, shepherds, pilgrims, peasants, and even animals and vineyards from warfare. In theory at least, the Peace of God exempted almost the entire population in Europe from violence and war. The peasants, who made up the majority population of Europe, were particularly vulnerable to violence. The Synod of Charroux in its *Proclamation of the Peace of God* (989 CE) provided special protection for the poor. We read:

> Anathema [excommunication] against those who rob the poor. If anyone robs a peasant or any other poor person of a sheep, ox, ass, cow, goat, or pig, let him be anathema until he makes satisfaction.

A great many of the restrictions in the Peace of God covered clerical persons and lands, and the censure on clerical participation in war was continued.

The Truce of God generally forbade war and violence from Wednesday evening to Monday morning, on saints' feast days, on holy days, and during such church seasons as Advent or Lent. The *Proclamation of the Truce at Besancon and Vienne* (ca. 1041 CE) was representative when it stated:

> We command all to keep the truce from sunset on Wednesday to sunrise on Monday, and from Christmas to the octave of Epiphany, and from Septuagesima Sunday to the octave of Easter.

The purpose of the Truce of God was to ensure that for a good period of the year clergy, merchants, and peasants could go about their duties secure in person and property. The Truce of God has not entirely vanished from history. It influenced, for example, the proposals of Pope Benedict XV (pope from 1914 to 1922) during World War I for a Christmas truce and for international arbitration to settle the dispute.

Roland Bainton in *Christian Attitudes toward War and Peace* records a remarkable union of the Peace of God with the Truce of God. These elements can be found in the Oath of King Robert II (ca. 970–1031) of France:

> I will not infringe on the Church in any way. I will not hurt a cleric or a monk if unarmed. I will not steal an ox, cow, pig, sheep, goat, ass, or a mare with colt. I will not attack a villain or villainess or servants or merchants for ransom. I will not take a mule of a horse, male or female, or a colt in pasture from any man from the calends of March to the feast of All Saints unless to recover a debt. I will not burn houses or destroy them unless there is a knight inside. I will not root up vines. I will not attack noble ladies traveling without husband nor their maids, nor widows or nuns unless it is their fault. From the beginning of Lent to the end of Easter I will not attack an unarmed knight.

The Peace of God and the Truce of God were, at times, undermined by the use of "peace militias" that, ironically, used violent means to enforce the restrictions. In addition, the Truce of God was invoked by Pope Urban II in his call to the Crusades in 1095. The "holy" or total wars that ensued against the Saracens (Muslims), in Urban's words "an accursed race, utterly alienated from God," relied heavily on maintaining the Truce of God in Europe.

The following points summarize the contribution of the *Penitential Books,* the Peace of God, and the Truce of God to the just war model:

- Killing in war is a sin for which soldiers must perform penance.
- Civilians may not be attacked in war.
- Clergy and church buildings may not be attacked.
- Violence may not be done to animals or to property.

A number of medieval theologians also contributed to the development of the just war model. For example, the Italian monk Gratian (ca. 1090–1155), who is credited with being the founder of "canon" or church law, held in his *Decretum (Decretals)* that wars could be "pacific" if they were fought for "the repression of the wicked and the deliverance of the good." The influence of the recently launched Crusades was evident in Gratian's statement that "whoever dies in battle against the infidels [Muslims] is worthy to enter the heavenly kingdom." Gratian repeated the more traditional restrictions of just war and held that soldiers who obey legitimate authority in war are not guilty of murder.

Alexander of Hales (ca. 1185–1245), an English Franciscan and professor at the University of Paris, identified several important conditions for a just war. They included the following: the war must be declared by a proper authority; the war must be fought with a proper intention; those warred upon must deserve to be attacked; and the war must be fought to support the good. Alexander preceded Thomas Aquinas at the University of Paris by just a few years. The writings of Thomas Aquinas, along with the writings of Augustine, are commonly used by those who hold that war is a legitimate—if limited—Christian enterprise. We turn now to a discussion of war in the thought of Thomas Aquinas.

Thomas Aquinas and Just War

Thomas Aquinas (1225–1274), a Dominican friar and professor at the University of Paris, discussed war in his famous work, *Summa Theologica* (Summary of Theology or *Summa*). Aquinas was writing in the context of the Crusades that had begun in 1095 and that dominated his own century, the thirteenth.

In this historical setting, it is interesting, therefore, that Aquinas places his discussion of war in the context of the theological virtues: faith, hope, and charity. War appears in the *Summa* under the heading "Charity" and it is presented as a "vice" (or defect) of charity. (Other vices of charity include hatred, discord, schism, strife, and sedition.) This is important because, like Augustine on whom he relies, Aquinas does not consider war to be a "virtue" in the sense that it is noble and glorious. Thus, even in the midst of the Crusades (when war was considered noble and glorious), Thomas Aquinas reminds the warriors of his day that military activity is based on a defect of charity. Clearly, war originates in sin; it is a failure to love.

Aquinas's reservations about war are evident even in the way he discusses the question of war. In the *Summa* (II-II, Q. 40, Art. 1) he asks: "Whether it is always sinful to wage war." Those who say "yes" to this question base their view, in part, on Matthew 26:52, "All who take the sword will perish by the sword," and on the medieval church's condemnation of "warlike exercises that take place in tournaments." (Note that the condemnation of tournaments can be traced to the condemnation of gladiatorial contests in the fourth-century *Theodosian Code*.)

Aquinas, however, holds that war is not "always" sinful. The exception is found in the just war. Aquinas states:

> I answer that for a war to be just, three things are necessary.
>
> First the authority of the sovereign by whose command the war is to be waged. For it is not the business of a private individual to declare war, because he can seek for redress of his rights from the tribunal of his superior....
>
> Secondly, a just cause is required, namely that those who are attacked should be attacked because they deserve it on account of some fault. Wherefore Augustine says: "A just war is wont to be described as one that avenges wrongs, when a nation or state has to be punished for refusing to make amends for the wrongs inflicted by its subjects or to restore what it has seized unjustly."
>
> Thirdly, it is necessary that the belligerents should have a rightful intention, so that they intend the advancement of good, or the avoidance of evil....For it may happen that the war is declared by the legitimate authority, and for a just cause, and yet be rendered unlawful through a wicked intention.

In his reply to those who hold that war is *always* sinful, Aquinas states that "it is necessary sometimes" to resist or engage in self-defense "for the common good, or for the good of those with whom [one] is fighting." It should be noted that Aquinas relies very heavily on Augustine in his discussion of the just war. (In the section from which the above quote is taken, for example, Augustine is quoted nine times; the sacred scriptures are quoted six times.) In a curious addition to his discussion on war, Aquinas asks, "Whether it is lawful to lay ambushes in war." His answer: Yes, laying ambushes to "conceal" one's strategy is permissible.

And what of "sedition" or revolution? Can citizens wage war against their own government? May the principles of the just war be used to violently overthrow a tyrannical king or government? Because Aquinas accepts Augustine's definition of peace as "the tranquility of order," he is hardly disposed to endorse "sedition" or even "strife," because both violate "good order." In addition, since civil and ecclesiastical authority are rooted in God's authority, Aquinas has a good deal of respect for them.

But Aquinas does recognize that a "tyrannical" abuse of power on the part of a government can justify revolution on the part of the subjects. There are several places in his writings where Aquinas examines the possibility of a "just" revolution and even "tyrannicide." They are found in the *Summa Theologica* (II-II, Q. 41) and in his treatise *On Kingship*. In *On Kingship* Aquinas states that "in cases where it belongs by right to a community to provide a ruler for itself, that community can without injustice depose or restrain a king whom it has appointed, if he should abuse royal power tyrannically."

The following points summarize the contribution of Thomas Aquinas to the just war model:

— War must be approved by a proper authority.
— War must have a just cause.
— War must be fought with the right intention.
— People have a right to depose a tyrant.

Perhaps because he bases much of his theology on Aristotle and on the philosophy of "natural law," Thomas Aquinas is more optimistic than Augustine about human nature and the possibility for peace. Therefore, running throughout both the letter and the spirit of Aquinas's writings is a presumption against violence as a corrective to social ills. Bloodshed isn't just a "last resort" for Aquinas; it is a failure to love—a failure to act as creatures who were created in God's image and redeemed by Jesus.

In *The Just War in Aquinas and Grotius,* Joan D. Tooke states: "To Aquinas, to kill in any way was in itself unjust. As war is nothing but the killing of men, in itself it must therefore be held unjust." Thomas Aquinas is well known for his teaching on just war. His *presumption against war*, however, is often forgotten.

Later Developments in the Just War Model

By the late Middle Ages, just war had become the official teaching of the Catholic Church and, in the sixteenth century, it became the teaching of the Reformers as well. Little that was new, however, was added to the principles of just war in the years to follow; most theologians and church leaders merely engaged in debate on how the principles were to be applied. Nevertheless, some of the thinkers and movements from the Reformation to our own time deserve to be mentioned.

The following people and events contributed to the refining of the just war model.

Luther and the Reformers. Martin Luther (1483–1546), an Augustinian monk, viewed war from the perspective of the "two kingdoms" doctrine. War, consequently, is an activity of the earthly, fallen kingdom, while peace is reserved to the spiritual kingdom of God. Luther subscribed to just war principles and believed—with certain restrictions—the military profession to be "a legitimate and godly calling and occupation." Luther especially stressed that only a legitimate authority may declare war.

Luther's teaching on war and peace had a strong influence on the many Reformers who came after him, some of whom embraced the concept of "holy" war. The wars of religion that followed the Reformation saw violations of just war principles by Protestant and Catholic alike. Other Reformers, such as the Anabaptists (discussed in the previous chapter), embraced pacifism

Christian Humanism. The humanists of the sixteenth century accepted the just war in varying degrees, but they interpreted just war in very restrictive terms. They were highly critical of the wars of their own time, whether led by pope or king. In the chapter on pacifism we discussed several of these humanists, including Desiderius

Erasmus of Rotterdam, John Colet and Thomas More of England, Juan Luis Vives of Spain, and Guillaume Bude of France.

A major contribution of the humanists was the introduction of a note of cynicism about why political leaders waged war. In his *Letter to Anthony Bergen* concerning the real "motives" for war, for example, Erasmus observes, "If you look narrowly into the case, you will find that they are, chiefly, the private, sinister, and selfish motives of princes which operate as the real causes of war." Thomas More in *Utopia* is equally skeptical: "In the first place, most princes are more interested in warfare . . . the acquisition of more territory by fair or foul means occupies them more than the wise administration of those they already possess."

Wars of Conquest and International Law. When Christopher Columbus set foot on what he thought were the outer islands of China in 1492, a series of events unfolded that resulted in the enslavement and massacre of the native people of the "New World." The wars of the Spanish Conquistadors (Conquerors) against the Indians were first justified on the grounds that the Indians had no "souls" and, therefore, were devoid of human rights. In addition, these wars were being fought "for God's glory."

Bartolomé de Las Casas (1474–1566), a former slave owner who became a Dominican friar, spoke vigorously for the human dignity of the Indians and persuaded the Catholic Church to accept the fact that they had souls. He influenced Pope Paul III to declare in 1537 that: (1) the Indians "are by no means to be deprived of their liberty," and (2) the Indians must be converted by "example of good and holy living"—not war.

Hence, a war that forced people to accept the Catholic faith (or a European way of life) could not be "just." Also, Las Casas held that the Spanish colonists who fought the "unjust wars" against the Indians were required to make restitution "to the devastated pagan peoples whatever they took in war." Las Casas's thinking was strongly influenced by Thomas Aquinas's teaching on "Restitution" in the *Summa Theologica*. Aquinas stated that a thief *and* the thief's commander (who may not have committed the actual theft) are bound to restitution. In Aquinas's words, "Whoever is cause of an unjust taking is bound to restitution."

Tommaso Cajetan (1469–1534), a Dominican philosopher whose *Commentary* on Aquinas' *Summa Theologica* is still in use today, also strongly influenced Las Casas's view that the invading Spaniards owed "restitution" to the Indians they had enslaved. Cajetan stated:

> So we would sin mortally if we sought to spread that faith of Christ by way of war. We would not be the legitimate rulers of the conquered, we would have committed a mighty theft, we should be held to restitution for being unjust aggressors in an unjust occupation.

Here we have the development of the "justice after war" *(ius post bellum)* concept. The traditional obligation to "repair injured rights" or to make restitution for stolen goods was extended by Cajetan to behavior in just war. Hence, a nation has a moral obligation to restore civil society and to rebuild the infrastructure of a nation it has attacked in violation of just war principles. Today, the principle of restitution is even extended to nations that legitimately defend themselves or others against attack (witness the U.S. Marshall Plan for reconstruction after World War II).

The international dimensions of the struggles in the New World led the Spanish Dominican Francisco de Vitoria (1492–1546) to hold that, based on universal human rights, the Indians were the natural possessors of the "New World." He also held that war could not be used to convert the Indians and that individuals had the right in conscience to refuse to serve in an unjust war.

In *On Civil Power*, Vitoria taught the principle of proportionality: a war is unjust if the evil outcome exceeds the good that may come from it. He also discussed the distinction between *"ius ad bellum"*— the right to go to war—and *"ius in bello"*—laws to be followed in war. Vitoria, along with the Spanish Jesuit Francisco Suarez (1548–1617), set the philosophical foundations for what was to become international law. We will discuss this more fully in the chapter on World Community.

The Dutch Protestant Hugo Grotius (1583–1645) is most famous for his *On the Law of War and Peace* (1625) in which he carefully explained just war in legal rather than theological terms. Concerning preventive or preemptive war, Grotius held that just war requires that a danger be "present and real," not remote or imaginary. In his words, "But to maintain that the bare probability of some remote or future annoyance from a neighboring state affords a just ground of hostile aggression is a doctrine repugnant to every principle of equity." Grotius advocated "conditional surrender" in war and held that arbitration and the recognition of international human rights could prevent wars in the future.

The centuries that followed saw the continued European conquest and colonization of the globe. Most of the European Christian countries, Protestant and Catholic alike, believed their expansionist policies to be "just" and, often, blessed by God. The just war model still existed as official teaching, but it was stretched almost beyond recognition. Slavery, torture, and rape were rationalized as "just" activities and the destruction of other cultures was sanctioned as having a divine mandate. Aside from the misuse of just war, little new was added until, with the invention of dynamite in the nineteenth century and nuclear weapons in the twentieth century, the question arose as to whether there could ever again be a just war.

Weapons of Mass Destruction and Just War

The concept of just war was devised in a time when a person could actually see, or at least hear, the person he killed. With the development of the crossbow, the importation of gun power from China, and the primitive artillery of the medieval period, the distinction between soldier (combatant) and civilian (non-combatant) began to vanish. Today, the accidental killing of civilians and even one's own soldiers is called "collateral damage" or "friendly fire" and is held by some to be morally acceptable if the direct intent is to kill only combatants. The killing of whole groups of people who cannot be seen is, of course, made possible by dynamite and other conventional weapons of extensive destruction.

The invention of dynamite in 1867 by Alfred Nobel (1833–1896) dramatically changed the size of the battlefield. The field increased from about a mile with gunpowder to over twenty miles with dynamite. As early as World War I (1914–1918), for example, Germany used the "Big Bertha," a cannon that could fire one-ton shells a distance of more than nine miles (fifteen kilometers). By World War II

(1939–1945), airplanes could bomb targets over a thousand miles away. The twentieth-century invention of nuclear, biological, and chemical (NBC) weapons along with their delivery systems (missiles, etc.) made first continents and then the whole world the battlefield. Today there is no safe place on earth from attack.

Advances in military technology have provided a severe challenge to morality in war. Can one fight a just war using weapons of mass destruction? Can a soldier in good conscience fire a weapon that he or she knows in advance will destroy whole villages and cities along with their populations? In short, has military technology destroyed military morality?

During World War II, bombing from the air was used by almost all belligerents: the Japanese bombed cities in China and the Philippines, the Germans bombed cities in England and Russia, the British bombed cities in Germany, and the Americans bombed cities in Germany and Japan.

At the beginning of the war, when Japan and Germany first bombed civilian populations, the American and British reacted with horror and charged that the bombing was "uncivilized," "inhumane," and "unjust." When the British and American governments changed their policy from "precision" to "saturation" or "obliteration" bombing and did exactly the same thing the Japanese and Germans were doing, few voices rose in protest.

One voice that did rise in protest was that of an English writer, Vera Brittain (1893–1970), who in 1944 wrote a pamphlet published by the Fellowship of Reconciliation entitled, *Massacre by Bombing: The Facts Behind the British-American Attack on Germany*. In *Massacre by Bombing* Brittain gives detailed accounts of the devastation of German cities by British and American bombers and concludes, "It seems there is nothing left except the war of all against all."

Massacre by Bombing influenced American moralist John C. Ford, SJ (1902–1989) in his article, "The Morality of Obliteration Bombing," published in 1944 in the Catholic journal *Theological Studies*. After a careful review of the concept of obliteration bombing and after examining several of the just war criteria, Fr. Ford concluded:

> Obliteration bombing, as defined, is an immoral attack on the rights of the innocent. It includes a direct intent to do

them injury. Even if this were not true, it would still be immoral, because no proportionate cause could justify the evil done; and to make it legitimate would soon lead the world to the immoral barbarity of total war....

Ford's article was to cause a stir among American Catholics, most of whom supported the war uncritically. Ford did, however, enjoy some support from the lay Catholic magazine *Commonweal* and another leading Catholic moralist, Paul Hanley Furfey.

Obviously, the same principles that were applied to the issue of obliteration bombing through conventional forces could be applied to the use of the atomic bombs that were dropped on Hiroshima and Nagasaki in 1945. Utilitarians (the "greatest good for the greatest number") debate how many lives were saved by the bombs, while other moralists use just war criteria to challenge the view that the direct killing of several hundred thousand civilians is an acceptable price to pay for peace.

This is, however, stretching the just war model far beyond its own reasonable limits. Nuclear and other weapons of mass destruction, due to their sheer size and capacity to destroy whole countries (and perhaps the planet), are properly understood as weapons of total war, which we will discuss in the next chapter.

Official Statements on Just War

The vast majority of the Christian churches support the just war model. Consequently, members of those churches may serve in the military. Soldiers and prospective soldiers should realize, however, that just war begins with "a strong presumption against the use of force." Therefore, there are important restrictions that most churches place on the right to go to war *(ius ad bellum),* what is morally permissible in war *(ius in bello),* and what happens after a war *(ius post bellum).* The formation of a "good" conscience on any matter pertaining to war should include careful reflection on the teaching of the church to which a person belongs along with consideration of other religious traditions and philosophical teachings.

The following are statements of several Christian churches on just war.

Methodist Council of Bishops (USA)

Some Christians support conventional military forces and remain open to the possible justice or necessary evil of some wars or revolutions but say No to all nuclear wars and weapons. For them the "nuclear threshold" is an absolute moral boundary that must never be crossed. They may appeal to the historic prerequisites of a "just war" in Christian tradition, such as proportionality and civilian immunity, in judging that nuclear weapons are too destructive ever to serve the ends of justice. (*In Defense of Creation: The Nuclear Crisis and a Just Peace*, 1986)

National Council of Churches USA

US unilateralism is accompanied by increasing militarism. Our government seems ready to use military means to confront its perceived adversaries, at times without exploring, much less exhausting, less violent policy options. It also increasingly tries to bend the world's will to its own through unilateral actions such as: withdrawing from the International Criminal Court (the first time any country has formally withdrawn its signature from such a convention); refusing to support UN peacekeeping operations until US armed forces were made exempt from the provisions of the ICC; withdrawing from efforts to agree on a verification protocol for the Biological Weapons Convention; and disregarding Geneva conventions for those captured in Afghanistan and detained at Guantanamo. (Background to General Assembly Resolution: "After September 11, 2001: Public Policy Considerations for the United States of America.")

Roman Catholic Church

Certainly, war has not been rooted out of human affairs. As long as the danger of war remains and there is no competent and sufficiently powerful authority at the international level, governments cannot be denied the right to legitimate defense once every means of peaceful settlement has been exhausted. Therefore, government authorities and others who share public responsibility have the duty to protect the welfare of the people entrusted to their care and to conduct such grave matters soberly.

But it is one thing to undertake military action for the just defense of the people, and something else again to seek the subjugation of other nations. Nor does the possession of war potential make every military or political use of it lawful. Neither does the mere fact that war has unhappily begun mean that all is fair between the warring parties.

Those who are pledged to the service of their country as members of its armed forces should regard themselves as agents of security and freedom on behalf of their people. As long as they fulfill this role properly, they are making a genuine contribution to the establishment of peace. (*Gaudium et Spes*: Pastoral Constitution on the Church in the Modern World, 1965, 79)

Catholic teaching begins in every case with a presumption against war and for peaceful settlement of disputes. In exceptional cases, determined by the moral principles of the just-war tradition, some uses of force are permitted. (United States National Conference of Catholic Bishops, A Pastoral Letter on War and Peace: *The Challenge of Peace: God's Promise and Our Response*, 1983, summary)

We remind all in authority and in the chain of command that their training and field manuals have long prohibited, and still do prohibit, certain actions in the conduct of war, especially those actions which inflict harm on innocent civilians. The question is not whether certain measures are unlawful or forbidden in warfare, but which measures: to refuse to take such actions is not an act of cowardice or treason but one of courage and patriotism.

We address particularly those involved in the exercise of authority over others. We are aware of your responsibilities and impressed by the standard of personal and professional duty you uphold. We feel, therefore, that we can urge you to do everything you can to assure that every peaceful alternative is exhausted before war is even remotely considered. In developing battle plans and weapons systems, we urge you to try to ensure that these are designed to reduce violence, destruction, suffering, and death to a minimum, keeping in mind especially non-combatants and other innocent persons. (*The Challenge of Peace*, 311-312)

We join with Pope John Paul in the conviction that war is not "inevitable" and that "war is always a defeat for humanity." This is not a matter of ends, but means. Our bishops' conference continues to question the moral legitimacy of any preemptive, unilateral use of military force to overthrow the government of Iraq. To permit preemptive or preventive uses of military force to overthrow threatening or hostile regimes would create deeply troubling moral and legal precedents. Based on the facts that are known, it is difficult to justify resort to war against Iraq, lacking clear and adequate evidence of an imminent attack of a grave nature or Iraq's involvement in the terrorist attacks of September 11. With the Holy See and many religious leaders throughout the world, we believe that resort to war would not meet the strict conditions in Catholic teaching for the use of military force. (United States Conference of Catholic Bishops, *Statement on Iraq*, Feb. 26, 2003)

The United Nations

Although not a religious body, the United Nations works closely with religious groups in their call for limitations on war. Its charter permits limited military action by member states for self-defense and to restore peace in other nations. We read in the UN Charter:

Article 42. Should the Security Council consider that [nonviolent] measures provided for in Article 41 would be inadequate or have proved to be inadequate, it may take such action by air, sea, or land forces as may be necessary to maintain or restore international peace and security. Such action may include demonstrations, blockade, and other operations by air, sea, or land forces of Members of the United Nations.

Article 51. Nothing in the present Charter shall impair the inherent right of individual or collective self-defence if an armed attack occurs against a Member of the United Nations, until the Security Council has taken measures necessary to maintain international peace and security. Measures taken by Members in the exercise of this right of self-defence shall be immediately reported to the Security Council and shall not in any way affect the authority and responsibility of the Security Council under the present Charter to take at any time such action as it deems necessary in order to maintain or restore international peace and security.

The Geneva Convention

The 1949 UN-sponsored Geneva Convention is a series of legally binding agreements that require humane treatment of "civilian persons in time of war" and of wounded and interned soldiers. The International Red Cross has played a central role in implementing the provisions of the Geneva Convention. Article 3 reads:

1. Persons [civilians] taking no active part in the hostilities, including members of armed forces who have laid down their arms and those placed hors de combat [disabled] by sickness, wounds, detention, or any other cause, shall in all circumstances be treated humanely, without any adverse distinction founded on race, color, religion or faith, sex, birth or wealth, or any other similar criteria.

To this end, the following acts are and shall remain prohibited at any time and in any place whatsoever with respect to the above-mentioned persons: (a) violence to life and person, in particular murder of all kinds, mutilation, cruel treatment and torture; (b) the taking of hostages; (3) outrages upon personal dignity, in particular humiliating and degrading treatment; (d) the passing of sentences and the carrying out of executions without previous judgment pronounced by a regularly constituted court, affording all the judicial guarantees which are recognized as indispensable by civilized peoples.

The United States is a signatory to the Geneva Convention.

Terrorism and Just War

The terrorist events of September 11, 2001, that killed almost three thousand people posed a severe challenge to the just war model. Just war advocates observed that the 9/11 attacks constituted an unjust attack on the United States and that a military response was necessary to defend the nation against further attack.

Advocates of just war recognized, however, that they were at a disadvantage in a war against terrorism for two reasons: (1) the terrorist attacks had been perpetrated by a non-state group that had found safe haven in many countries, few of which endorsed terrorism; and (2) there could be only a *limited* response against an enemy that recognized no limits on warfare. In other words, this was an "asymmetrical" war: a state was fighting a non-state enemy, and it was bound to respect just war principles while the terrorists were not. Nevertheless, just war advocates believed that the war against terrorism could be successfully fought within the limits on military action that were imposed by just war principles.

A just war response to terrorism endorses:

- *War as a last resort.* Terrorists often count on a strong military response to their terrorist acts to convince people that in fact the *other* side is the "militarist" group or nation. Military action, therefore, should be taken only after all diplomatic and international resources have been exhausted. Equally important is the necessity to act morally and legally by securing national and international support for military action.

- *Proportionality.* The good to be achieved from military action in response to terrorism must outweigh the evil that will be inflicted. Stated another way, if it becomes apparent that a military response will result in far greater damage than was caused by a terrorist act, there is a duty to refrain from or severely modify military action. Revenge may not be a motive in military action.

- *Just conduct.* Preemptive military strikes of a limited ("surgical") nature are permitted if there is absolute certainty that a terrorist attack is imminent. Terrorists, whether they are considered military personnel or criminals, are the only legitimate military targets. Military strikes or attacks on suspected terrorist targets must take every precaution to avoid killing the innocent. Captured terrorists—soldiers or civilians—are entitled to legal protection and humane living conditions. Physical and psychological torture and sexual abuse are forbidden.

- *Just termination.* In order to enhance the greater good, communication with terrorist organizations should be pursued with a view to negotiating a just settlement that disarms the terrorists *and* addresses the causes of terrorist behavior. The use of mediation and arbitration at local and international levels may be effective methods in ending terrorist activity. Restitution should be required for military activity that has injured the innocent.

Conclusion

The just war model was never meant to justify war. It was meant to limit war, to control war, and even to avoid war. Even before the just war model was reluctantly accepted by Christians, most ancients held that war was to be fought with regret, with sadness.

Shedding the blood of an enemy is never meant to be an occasion for joy. For we become as we behave, and when we kill another we slowly but surely kill ourselves. Peace is a worthy end, but war as a means to it must always be a last resort and subject to the strictest of moral conditions. In fact, even some just war advocates hold that war is the lesser of two evils, but an evil nonetheless. The ancients knew this and the early Christians did as well. That is why killing in war required forgiveness and penance throughout the first thousand years of Christian history.

Just war advocates think it is terribly important to keep these "limitations" imposed by the just war model in mind, especially in our own time, when more and more aspects of war are being accepted as legitimate. Killing children is justified, destroying the environment is justified, torturing prisoners is justified, denying civil liberties is justified, and weapons of mass destruction that can destroy whole countries are justified. Offensive wars that "preempt" or "prevent" future wars, and wars fought for empire are held by some to be morally just.

As the centuries have gone by and as the technology of war has made possible the death of millions in an instant, critics of the just war model have stated that it is "obsolete" and should be relegated to the trash bin of history. Others respond that this would leave contemporary war entirely without a moral compass. The just war model is still relevant, they contend, and must continue to be applied in the debate that leads to war, and to the question of what tactics and weapons are to be used in war.

Hence, it remains critically important that the just war model be taught at war colleges, at military academies, and, especially, to those civilian officials who will have the authority to declare a war but who will not personally fight in it. All must continually ask themselves, "Have we done everything to prevent war? Is this *really* a last resort? Are we needlessly wasting the lives of our soldiers? Are even our precision targets killing innocent people? Are we filled with hatred and revenge? How will history judge us?" Perhaps the chief contribution of the just war model is to ensure that a measure of remorse remains foundational to all discussion and training that prepare for war.

The Just War Model: A Summary

These are key points that characterize the just war model:

1. Coercion is necessary in human affairs. While human beings can live in peace, there are times when war—as a last resort—must be used to defend innocent people. Police and soldiers are foundational to a well-ordered society; armed force is necessary in human affairs.

2. War requires a just cause. A nation must defend itself through nonviolent civilian resistance, or through the use of armed forces, in case of invasion or attack. When diplomacy fails, nations may intervene to protect the innocent in other nations. Citizens may rebel against an illegitimate government to restore violated rights. War may not be fought to acquire territory or to dominate others.

3. War must be a last resort. All peaceful alternatives must be exhausted before lethal force is used. Informal and formal attempts at conciliation, mediation, and arbitration at national *and* international levels must have failed before war is declared. Military peacekeeping centers and civilian peace institutions should be consulted before going to war.

4. War must be declared by a legitimate authority. A nation's decision to commit military troops or engage in combat must be grounded in its national constitutions and in international law (i.e., the United Nations Charter). Executive authority alone is insufficient to validly declare war. Even a legally declared war may become unjust if a nation's citizens clearly speak out and vote against it.

5. War must be fought with the right intention. The intention of war must be to restore peace or to defend violated rights, not to destroy the enemy. Wars may not be fought for revenge or to settle grudges. Wars should also be fought with a view to "negotiated" peace; surrender must be conditional, not unconditional. Hence, the "demonization" of the enemy is forbidden.

6. Conscience must be respected. National and international law must respect the consciences of those civilians and soldiers who refuse to participate in war for moral reasons. Citizens who dissent from the general consensus for war should be regarded as honorable patriots. Soldiers should be properly instructed in the laws of war and of proper conduct in combat.

7. There must be a strong probability of success. Strategists who plan wars, and the military commanders who execute those wars, must have virtual certainty that military action will restore or establish peace. If a war cannot be won, it should not be fought.

8. Conduct in war must be just. Only active military combatants are legitimate targets in war. Noncombatants—civilians, captured soldiers, and medical personnel—must be treated in a humane fashion. Civilians may not be used as hostages and women must be protected against rape. Prisoners must not be tortured. Property and environmental damage must be minimal. Civilian and military commanders may not order soldiers to violate the rules of war.

9. Proportionality: The good must outweigh the evil. If, as a war progresses, it becomes evident that destruction of human life (and the environment) at the war's end will far exceed any good that can be achieved, the war must stop. Weapons of mass destruction—nuclear, biological, and chemical (NBC) weapons—are not permitted, since the suffering they will cause will outweigh any positive benefit.

10. The war must be justly terminated and restitution must be made. The just termination of a war requires a negotiated ("conditional") surrender that includes: immunity for soldiers of lower rank; continuation of police and governmental functions; legal representation for those accused or suspected of war crimes; and the right to international assistance from such organizations as the Red Cross. The victor in war has a moral obligation to make restitution for damage that was done to civil society and the nation's infrastructure.

———— • ————

Nicole needs your help in understanding the just war model. Write her a letter in which you answer the following questions:

1. What is the biblical basis for just war?

2. Why did Christianity embrace the concept of just war?

3. What medieval limitations were place on warfare?

4. How does the just war model respond to terrorism?

5. What, in your opinion, are the three most important key points in the just war model?

You can finish your letter by stating your own views on just war. You might discuss what you consider to be its strong points and weak points.

Your letter will be helpful to Nicole as she struggles to form her conscience on war. But neither you nor she will be able to take an intelligent stand on war until you work your way through the next two chapters on total war and World Community.

Recommended Reading

The following books are recommended if you would like to learn more about just war:

Shannon E. French. *Code of the Warrior: Exploring Warrior Values Past and Present*. Rowman & Littlefield Publishers, 2003.

James Turner Johnson. *Morality and Contemporary Warfare*. Yale University Press, 1999.

Terry Nardin, ed. *The Ethics of War and Peace: Religious and Secular Perspectives*. Princeton University Press, 1996.

Joan D. Tooke. *The Just War in Aquinas and Grotius*. London: S.P.C.K., 1965.

Michael Waltzer. *Just and Unjust Wars: A Moral Argument with Historical Illustrations*. Basic Books, 1977.

Daniel S. Zupan. *War, Morality and Autonomy: An Investigation in Just War Theory*. Ashgate Publishing, 2004.

Total War

*"This is not an enemy we can reason with,
or negotiate with, or appease.
This is, to put it simply,
an enemy that must be vanquished."*
Richard Cheney

Introduction

Total war is a social philosophy which holds that human society is in a perpetual state of war and that victory in war requires the annihilation of enemies.

This model, therefore, differs substantially from the just war model in its presumption that human society is in a "perpetual state of war." The just war model acknowledges that war is a social reality, but does not believe it is "perpetual" in human affairs, since, after all, it dates only to beginnings of territoriality (agriculture) about ten thousand years ago.

According to the just war model, wars occur in human history, but they are not the *essence* of human history, as total war proponents allege. Nor, despite the superficial view of history that contends they are the "stuff" of history, are wars very common. Proponents of just war hold that war is in fact the exception in human affairs and war has been, and can be, avoided.

Since the just war model seeks to impose moral "limits" on the conduct of war, another major difference between total war and just war has to do with the issue of "annihilation of enemies." Annihilation means the indiscriminate destruction of one's foe. Just war philosophy is rooted in the conviction that there is a moral presumption *against* war, while the total war position rests on a moral presumption *for* war. Hence, it is a very high violation of the ethical code of just war to engage in indiscriminate killing, while in the total war model such behavior is acceptable and could even be considered praiseworthy.

Another substantial difference between just war and total war lies in the notion of virility and warfare. Proponents of just war believe that men do, of course, fight and kill, but that their intention must be to protect innocent life and to restore the peace. As we have seen, for almost a thousand years of Christian history penance was required of those who had killed in battle because killing even in a "just" war was still regarded as evil. Once total war became the norm in Christian history in the form of the Crusades, however, warriors who killed indiscriminately in battle were considered noble men, heroes meriting divine forgiveness of sin and public acclaim. In the medieval period, "real men" went off to war and took no prisoners, all in the name of God. Virility and violence were linked and now enjoyed divine support.

In a religious context, "holy war" is another name for total war. As we shall see, holy wars are wars fought "in God's name, for God's glory, and for God's gain." The notion that God is a warrior (or that there are warrior gods) is quite old in human history. Far from being only a symbol of our barbarous past, it is a notion that remains with us today. Holy warriors contend that war is God's act of judgment on a sinful human race; holy war is God's total war against the demonic forces of evil. We turn now to a discussion of total war—holy war—in the Bible.

Holy War in the Hebrew Scriptures

As we have seen in earlier chapters, the Hebrew Scriptures contain many passages that speak of peace and nonviolence, and some passages that relate to just war. The concept of total or holy war also appears in the Hebrew Scriptures. The following example from the Bible highlights the notion that wars are properly God's activity and that they are indiscriminate. In Deuteronomy we read:

When you go out to war against your enemies, and see horses and chariots, an army larger than your own, you shall not be afraid of them; for the LORD your God is with you, who brought you up from the land of Egypt. Before you engage in battle, the priest shall come forward and speak to the troops, and shall say to them: "Hear, O Israel! Today you are drawing near to do battle against your enemies. Do not lose heart, or be afraid, or panic, or be in dread of them; for it is the LORD your God who goes with you, to fight for you against your enemies, to give you victory. (Deuteronomy 20:1–4)

But as for the towns of these peoples that the LORD your God is giving you as an inheritance, you must not let anything that breathes remain alive. You shall annihilate them—the Hittites and the Amorites, the Canaanites and the Perizzites, the Hivites and the Jebusites—just as the LORD your God has commanded, so that they may not teach you to do all the abhorrent things that they do for their gods, and you thus sin against the LORD your God. (Deuteronomy 20:16–18)

Another reference to holy war can be found in the Book of Joshua:

When Israel had finished slaughtering all the inhabitants of Ai in the open wilderness where they pursued them, and when all of them to the very last had fallen by the edge of the sword, all Israel returned to Ai, and attacked it with the edge of the sword. The total of those who fell that day, both men and women, was twelve thousand—all the people of Ai. For Joshua did not draw back his hand, with which he stretched out the sword, until he had utterly destroyed all the inhabitants of Ai. Only the livestock and the spoil of that city Israel took as their booty, according to the word of the LORD that he had issued to Joshua. So Joshua burned Ai, and made it forever a heap of ruins, as it is to this day. (Joshua 8:24–28)

These passages refer to the Jewish people seizing the land—the "inheritance"—that had been promised by their God. Unlike just war, holy war is not a "sorrowful" activity and mercy is not to be shown to Israel's enemies.

It is important to see these passages in their historical context. The God of Israel at this point is a "warrior" God who takes great measures to ensure that the Jewish people know they do not fight their wars alone—that God fights for them (see Deuteronomy 20:1–9).

The holy war ethic was not unique to the Jews; it was also found in surrounding cultures of the time.

Holy War in the Christian Scriptures

The passages in the Christian Scriptures that are offered to justify participation in war for Christians were examined in the previous chapter on just war. These passages are "foundational" passages that are also used to make the case for Christian holy war. Those who make the case for holy war in Christian terms urge people to recall that even in the "New" Testament we still find a God of wrath, punishment, and vengeance.

The Book of Revelation (sometimes called the "Apocalypse") is the Christian book that is most often used to justify holy war for Christians. Revelation deals with God's final victory over evil and is perhaps best known for the "four horsemen of the Apocalypse" found in Revelation 6: War, Famine, Pestilence, and Death. Chapter 19 describes the victory of the heavenly armies over the "beast," which symbolizes all that is not Christian. We read:

> Then I saw heaven opened, and there was a white horse! Its rider is called Faithful and True, and in righteousness he judges and makes war. His eyes are like a flame of fire, and on his head are many diadems; and he has a name inscribed that no one knows but himself. He is clothed in a robe dipped in blood, and his name is called The Word of God. And the armies of heaven, wearing fine linen, white and pure, were following him on white horses. From his mouth comes a sharp sword with which to strike down the nations, and he will rule them with a rod of iron; he will tread the wine press of the fury of the wrath of God the Almighty. On his robe and on his thigh he has a name inscribed, "King of kings and Lord of lords."

Then I saw an angel standing in the sun, and with a loud voice he called to all the birds that fly in midheaven, "Come gather for the great supper of God, to eat the flesh of kings, the flesh of captains, the flesh of the mighty, the flesh of horses and their riders—flesh of all, both free and slave, both small and great." Then I saw the beast and the kings of the earth with their armies gathered to make war against the rider on the horse and against his army. And the beast was captured and with it the false prophet who had performed in its presence the signs by which he deceived those who had received the mark of the beast and those who worshiped its image. These two were thrown alive into the lake of fire that burns with sulfur. And the rest were killed by the sword of the rider on the horse, the sword that came from his mouth; and all the birds were gorged with their flesh. (Revelation 19:11–21)

Revelation 20:4 relates that those "who had not worshiped the beast...came to life and reigned with Christ a thousand years." After this, a final battle will take place between the Christians and the forces of Satan. We read:

When the thousand years are ended, Satan will be released from his prison and will come out to deceive the nations at the four corners of the earth, Gog and Magog, in order to gather them for battle; they are as numerous as the sands of the sea. They marched over the breadth of the earth and surrounded the camp of the saints and the beloved city. And fire came down from heaven and consumed them. And the devil who had deceived them was thrown into the lake of fire and sulfur, where the beast and the false prophet were, and they will be tormented day and night forever and ever. (Revelation 20:7–10)

These and other passages from Revelation describe the "second coming," when Jesus Christ will return to earth and inaugurate the "end times." When this happens, the "righteous" will be taken up bodily to Heaven in the "rapture." After this, the "great tribulation" will last for seven years, during which Christ and the "saints" will form an army and defeat the beast and the forces of evil. Christ will then rule in peace for a thousand years ("Christian millennialism"). When this period has ended, Satan will return to fight the final battle with Christ. Satan will lose this battle and be condemned to Hell forever. Following this, the "last judgment" will take place and God will reward good people with Paradise and consign evil people to Hell.

Those who interpret the Bible literally anticipate that a "cosmic war" is inevitable before the final judgment when Christ will rule in all his glory. Hence, there is widespread anticipation of a Christian "total war" in which Satan will be conquered and evil people will be punished. Violence and destruction have an important place in the theology of fundamentalist Christians who adhere to a literal interpretation of the Bible. The popular "Left Behind" series is based on such theology.

Biblical scholars and theologians, however, caution that one can use isolated texts and passages from the Bible to justify almost anything. Consequently, the passages that seem to justify total war can also be accurately interpreted as referring to a kind of "spiritual" or symbolic war—especially when such passages are read in the context of the rest of the New Testament. Nevertheless, the foundation for divinely ordained war and punishment is there. It certainly has been used, and continues to be used, by those who advocate holy war.

The following perspectives on holy war can be found in the Hebrew and Christian Scriptures:

- God is a warrior who fights for the Jewish people.
- God's people may seize the land of others as their own.
- Enemies are to be annihilated or damned.
- God's armies will conquer the forces of evil.
- The good are rewarded with Paradise; Hell awaits evil people.

These perspectives obviously stand in rather stark contrast to those that were examined in the chapter on pacifism, and even the chapter on just war. They form the foundation for what was to be the third major historical expression of the Christian tradition on war and peace: the Crusades. The Crusades mark the entrance into Christian history of total war as expressed through holy war.

The Crusades: God's Wars

The Crusades inaugurated a marked change in both the theological foundation and the political orientation of Catholic Europe, a change that in the centuries that followed was to have great impact on much of the world. Although the church did not know it at the time, these holy wars signaled as dramatic a shift in Christian life in the eleventh century as did the shift to just war in the fifth century.

The word "Crusade" is derived from the Latin word *crux,* which means cross. Crusaders wore a bright red cross (white and green were also used) on the front of their garments when they left for the Crusades and on the back of their garments when they returned. (To this day, therefore, the followers of Islam see in the cross an image of militarism.) The causes of the Crusades are, of course, quite complex and include important theological, spiritual, ecclesiastical, political, and economic factors. The following are among the most important:

Pessimistic Theology. The theology of original sin as formulated by Augustine of Hippo in the early fifth century held that "fallen" human beings were "depraved" from birth because they were lacking the saving "grace" of God. Even after baptism, people still exhibited signs of depravity and, hence, lust, greed, and violence characterized humankind. War, therefore, was inevitable in this "earthly city." Gradually, Christian warriors came to see themselves as instruments of God's wrath here on earth.

The Just War Tradition. After the fifth century, participation in warfare on the part of Christians became acceptable, first to spread the *Pax Christiana* through the *Pax Romana,* second to defend against "barbarian" attacks, and third to defend the church itself against heresy. Nevertheless, nonviolence, compromise, and accommodation were often used to settle disputes, and after wars had been fought Christian soldiers were expected to do penance for having killed in war. Once war, however limited, was accepted as a Christian enterprise, the lines between "legitimate" and "illegitimate" behavior slowly but surely became blurred.

The Holy Roman Empire. In 800 CE Charles the Great (Charlemagne) became emperor of the reconstituted "Holy" Roman Empire. Papal support was required for his appointment, since the Catholic Church had great power in the civil realm. In the centuries that followed, however, despite the church's influence and the existence of the Holy Roman Empire, Europe was basically in a state of political anarchy. The Crusades helped to end this anarchy by unifying Europe against a common enemy: Islam.

Mercenaries. Because there were no civilian standing armies in the Middle Ages, kings and princes relied on soldiers for hire ("soldiers of fortune") to fight their wars or to settle their differences. The mercenaries, however, were little more than bands of hoodlums who often fought with each other and endangered the lives of the common people and the clergy. The rise of the fabled medieval warrior horsemen known as knights resulted from a reform movement in reaction to these "freelance companies." The knights' code of honor of "chivalry" elevated mercenaries to the status of "professional" soldiers by requiring that knights honor the restrictions of the Peace of God and the Truce of God. Knights—and warrior monastic orders of knights—were to feature prominently in the Crusades.

The Saracen "Menace." In the medieval period, Muslims were called "Saracens." Although some Christians had peaceful relations with the Muslims, and many knew nothing of them, other Christians considered them to be, in Pope Urban II's words, "an accursed race, utterly alienated from God." The Arabs, Berbers, Kurds, and Turks who made up the Muslim population had controlled much of the land in the Middle East and Asia Minor, including Christian pilgrimage sites, since well before the seventh century. Regaining control of the Christian holy places in the Middle East was a prime motivation for the Crusades.

In 1071 the Seljuk Turks captured Jerusalem and proceeded to profane the holy places in Palestine and to persecute, rob, and beat Christian pilgrims. Fearing that the Turks would capture Constantinople as well, the Byzantine emperor Alexius Comnenus sought military assistance from Pope Urban II. This invitation, together with other difficulties that existed between Catholics and Muslims, provided a perfect opportunity to declare a "holy war" against the "infidels."

It should be stressed, however, that Muslims, Jews, and Christians had lived peacefully with each other in such diverse places as Spain and Jerusalem for hundreds of years prior to the Crusades. As all Muslims came to be judged by the behavior of the few, so all Muslims became the target of misunderstanding and hatred. Conversely, especially as the Crusades intensified, many Muslims came to regard Christians in a similarly negative fashion. Indeed, significant numbers on both sides continue to regard each other with mistrust to this day. The characterization of an entire religion or ethnic group of people as a "different race," or a "vile race," or as "infidels," or "pagans," or "evil" is the first step to holy war. Our words are intimately connected with our actions.

In 1095 at the Council of Clermont in France, Pope Urban II (ca. 1040–1099, pope from 1088 to 1099) issued a historic call, stating:

> Oh, what a disgrace if a race [Islam] so despised, degenerate, and slave of the demons should thus conquer a people fortified with faith in the omnipotent God and resplendent with the name of Christ! Oh, how many reproaches will be heaped upon you by the Lord himself if you do not aid those who like yourselves are counted of the Christian faith!
>
> Let those who have formerly been accustomed to contend wickedly in private warfare against the faithful fight against the infidel and bring to a victorious end the war which ought long since to have been begun. Let those who have hitherto been robbers now become soldiers of Christ. Let those who have formerly contended against their brothers and relatives now fight as they ought against the barbarians. Let those who have formerly been mercenaries at low wages now gain eternal rewards. Let those who have been striving to the detriment both of body and soul now labor for a twofold reward.
>
> What shall I add? On this side will be the sorrowful and poor, on the other the joyful and rich; here the enemies of the Lord, there his friends. Let not those who are going delay their journey, but having arranged their affairs and collected the money necessary for their expenses, when the

winter ends and the spring comes, let them with alacrity start
on their journey under the guidance of the Lord.

To this the assembly reportedly cried, "Deus Vult!" ("God wills it!")
and there was rejoicing that, at last, peace could return to Europe
through fighting the "infidel" abroad. Before long, this holy war
preached by Urban II became known as a "Crusade" after those who
"took up the cross" by placing "on their breasts the sign of the
quickening cross."

The Crusaders were granted several "privileges" as rewards for
their military service. These included: (1) a papal indulgence (forgiveness) for the "full remission" of sins upon taking a *votum crucis*
(vow) to go on a Crusade; (2) the ability to "send suitable men at
their expense" as substitutes on a Crusade; and, while they were on a
Crusade, (3) papal protection of their families and property; (4) a
moratorium on payment of debts and interest on debts; and (5) a sus-
pension of civil trials. The papal indulgence was especially attrac-
tive, since it meant that one who died in battle (or on the way to
battle) would immediately go to Heaven.

The call to the Crusades was, of course, rooted in the just war
appeal to "defend the Christians" who were being persecuted by the
Muslims in the Middle East. Many Christians regarded the Muslim
residents in Jerusalem and other holy places as illegal occupiers of
territory that properly belonged to Christians. Hence, in their view,
they were rightly defending land that constituted their spiritual
legacy. Further, advocates for a holy war against the Muslims
pointed out that Islam was, in essence, a "military" religion that had
spread across the Middle East and Africa and into Spain in the
eighth century through forced conversion and war. Islam had to be
stopped and destroyed before it attacked Europe again. Hence, the
defense of Europe justified a preemptive attack.

The Crusades, however, also served other purposes: (1) the Crusades dramatically increased the power of the papacy over European
civil affairs; (2) the Crusades provided an opportunity to seize territory in the Byzantine East (that had split from the papacy in 1054);
and (3) the Crusades opened new trade routes that provided access to
the wealth of the East. Thus, though the Crusades against Islam were
largely military failures, they were quite successful in the political
and economic realms.

The Crusades were truly egalitarian in nature, as kings and princes, knights and merchants, monks and priests, peasants and servants, and whole families went off to war. Women participated as warriors in several Crusades—Eleanor of Acquitaine (ca. 1122–1204) is most famous—while women at home assumed traditional male roles—Blanche of Castile (1187–1251), for example, ruled France. The poor were especially attracted to the Crusades as a way of escaping their misery and gaining salvation.

A series of eight major Crusades against Islam were fought between 1095 and 1291 when Acre, the last of the Christian territories in Palestine, was lost. During this period there were also numerous minor Crusades as well as two "Children's Crusades" of 1212. The children on these Crusades never reached Jerusalem; they either drowned en route or were sold into slavery.

The question might be asked, "Why so many Crusades?" The answer is simple: because they almost all failed. While there were territorial gains in the First and Third Crusades, these did not last. Each time a Crusading army attacked the Middle East and gained a foothold, the forces of Islam rose up to drive them out. Some of these wars were total wars against the "Christian infidels," while others followed the just war tradition, with victorious commanders allowing defeated forces to retreat, thus showing mercy to their Christian foes.

Perhaps the most famous of the Islamic leaders who repulsed the Christians was Saladin (1148–1193), a Kurd born in Tikrit (Iraq). After Saladin captured Jerusalem from the Crusaders in 1187, the Crusaders were never again able to dominate the Arab world. Settlements would remain, but the loss of Crusader territory was permanent. However, because Saladin had allowed enemy soldiers and knights to retreat instead of killing them, many of these Christian soldiers participated in yet another Crusade to try *again* to capture Jerusalem.

This was the Third Crusade (1189–1192), led in part by Richard "The Lion-Hearted," of Britain. It failed to recapture Jerusalem but had other territorial successes. In a peace treaty with the Crusaders, Saladin permitted their safe withdrawal and the resumption of pilgrimages to Jerusalem. Saladin's triumph against the Christian forces many centuries ago, however, remains very much alive in the memory of today's Muslims.

Voices from the Crusades

What follows is a very small sample of voices from the Crusades. These voices express the attitude that some Christians had toward the medieval holy wars.

Raymond d'Aguiliers. Raymond d'Aguiliers, chronicler of the First Crusade, provides a vivid account of the fall of Jerusalem in 1099:

> But now that our men had possession of the walls and towers, wonderful sights were to be seen. Some of our men (and this was more merciful) cut off the heads of their enemies; others shot them with arrows, so that they fell from the towers; others tortured them longer by casting them into the flames. Piles of heads, hands, and feet were to be seen in the streets of the city. It was necessary to pick one's way over the bodies of men and horses.
>
> But these were small matters compared to what happened at the temple of Solomon, a place where religious services are normally chanted. What happened there? If I tell the truth, it will exceed your powers of belief. So let it suffice to say this much, at least, that in the Temple and porch of Solomon, men rode in blood up to their knees and bridle reins. Indeed, it was a just and splendid judgment of God that this place should be filled with the blood of the unbelievers, since it had suffered so long from their blasphemies. The city was filled with corpses and blood.
>
> This day, I say, will be famous in all future ages, for it turned our labors and sorrows into joy and exultation; this day, I say, marks the justification of all Christianity, the humiliation of paganism, and the renewal of our faith. "This is the day which the Lord hath made, let us rejoice and be glad in it," for on this day the Lord revealed Himself to his people and blessed them.

Bernard of Clairvaux. A Cistercian monk, Bernard of Clairvaux (1090–1153), preached the Second Crusade (1147–1149). Note his reference to "martyrs in battle":

Go forward, therefore, in confidence, O Knights, and with dauntless spirit drive out the enemies of the cross of Christ. Be certain that neither death nor life can divorce you from the love of God, which is in Christ Jesus. In all danger repeat this within yourselves: "Whether we live or whether we die, we are the Lord's" [Romans 14:8]. With what happiness they die, martyrs in battle!

Catherine of Siena. Saint and doctor of the church, Catherine of Siena (1347–1380) believed the Crusades would bring unity at home and liberation to the souls of the infidels. Catherine believed that Christians had a duty to shed their blood for Christ who had shed his blood for them: "Fire up your desire to pay blood for blood." Here is an excerpt from a letter she wrote to a mercenary of the time:

Then you would be one of Christ's company, going to fight the unbelieving dogs who have possession of our holy place, where gentle First Truth lived and endured sufferings and death for us. You find so much satisfaction in fighting and waging war, so now I am begging you tenderly in Christ Jesus not to wage war any longer against Christians (for that offends God), but to go instead to fight the unbelievers, as God and our Holy Father decreed. How cruel it is that we who are Christians, members bound together in the body of holy Church, should be persecuting one another.

Catherine strikes a common theme throughout history's wars: war abroad demands unity at home.

Space does not permit the inclusion of more voices from the Crusades, but divine wrath and the punishment of "infidels" are common themes that run through these holy wars.

Since this chapter examines the development of total war in Christian history, important Muslim voices from the Crusades are not included. The interested reader may, however, wish to consult Amin Maalouf's *The Crusades through Arab Eyes* (Schocken, 1984) for Muslim perspectives on the Christian holy wars.

Also missing here are the voices of the average soldier, his wife, his children, and his friends at home. We have few written records of the words of these people. What must they have felt and experienced? As with most wars until the modern period, the only voices we hear are those of either the leaders or generals, few of whom saw combat. Their words, like compendiums of cold statistics and chronological listings of events, do not reveal the human face of war.

The following perspectives on total war as holy war can be found in the Crusades:

- Society is in a perpetual state of war.
- Holy war is fought for God's glory.
- All sins are forgiven to those who fight in God's name.
- Those who die in war go straight to Heaven.
- Killing enemies liberates them from their sins.
- Preemptive war is a duty.
- Indiscriminate killing in holy war is legitimate.

Military Religious Orders

Even after laypeople could legitimately shed blood in war after the fifth century, priests and monks were exempted from military service because their calling was to "spiritual" rather than "corporal" matters. A major change, therefore, took place when religious orders of monks founded at the time of the Crusades assumed military roles. These were orders of "Christian knights" (sometimes called "warrior monks") who took the traditional monastic vows of poverty, chastity, and obedience. In addition to performing military duties, the monks cared for pilgrims and supervised hospitals for the sick. An exception was the Carmelite friars, the only religious order without a military function founded in the Crusader states.

The three most prominent of the military orders were: the Poor Knights of Christ (Knights Templar), the Hospitallers of St. John of Jerusalem (Knights of Malta), and the Teutonic Knights (the "German Order"). A word about each:

Poor Knights of Christ (Knights Templar). The Templars, founded in Jerusalem in 1119, were originally military escorts to pilgrims to the Holy Land. Eventually they erected fortresses in many of the Crusader states and became defenders against attacks by Muslims. They developed a highly efficient banking system and amassed great wealth and power. In 1312, because of allegations of corruption, the order was dissolved by Pope Clement V and their wealth and property were transferred to their rivals, the Hospitallers.

Hospitallers. These knights, known today as Knights of Malta, were originally founded to perform charitable works. In 1113 Pope Paschal II recognized the order and it increasingly took on a military role so that by 1200 it was primarily a military order. With the fall of Palestine in 1291, the order moved to Rhodes and eventually to Malta. Over time it abandoned military affairs and returned to charitable works. Composed mainly of aristocrats, the Knights strongly support the Catholic Church and are noted for anti-Communist activities.

Teutonic Knights. Known today as the "German Order," this order of German noblemen was founded in Palestine in 1190 to serve in a hospital but it soon became a military order to fight the Turks in the Holy Land. Pope Innocent III recognized the order in 1199 and it later moved to Eastern Europe, where its members waged war against the Slavs and conquered Prussia. They joined forces with the Order of the Brothers of the Sword in 1237, but over time their influence waned and their rule in Prussia ended after 1525 with the Protestant Reform. In the 1930s some National Socialists in Germany used the memory of the Teutonic Knights to justify the Nazi conquest of Eastern Europe.

There were many other orders of knights, both religious and secular, that were founded at the time of the Crusades. Although the military monastic orders did not last as warriors, they did demonstrate that the line between monk and laity had been crossed so that even monks and clergy could kill in war. As time went on, even popes (such as Julius II, who was pope from 1503 to 1513) had armies and led men into battle.

The Inquisitions: Crusades at Home

The Crusades abroad provided a context in which to launch Crusades at home—called "inquisitions"—against heretics, dissidents, and women.

Christianity had dealt with the question of heresy from its earliest years. Throughout history, sincere Christians have disagreed with each other on many matters. When the matter in question has to do with official church doctrine, dissent from that doctrine is considered by the church to be heresy. The church's way of dealing with heretics in the early centuries was through excommunication, which means exclusion from the rights of church membership.

After the church gained some measure of worldly power in the fourth century, ecclesiastical officials became increasingly concerned with purging the church of theological dissidents and the bishops began to employ civil authority to punish or persecute heretics. This was especially true in one of the great controversies that changed the direction of Christian history: that between the Pelagians and Augustine of Hippo in the early fifth century. The death penalty was not used to persecute heretics, however, since it was thought to be irreconcilable with the Christian message of forgiveness and love of enemies.

This was to change at the time of the Crusades. The Crusades were launched—as we have seen above—against the Saracen "infidels." It was no great stretch to see a parallel between infidels abroad and heretics at home. Essentially, church leaders saw no difference between these two "enemies of the faith."

In the early part of the thirteenth century, Pope Innocent III declared a Crusade against the Albigenses in southern France. The Albigenses (also known as Cathari) were largely a pacifist Christian sect that was seen as heretical. The Crusade against them was conducted in the spirit of and used the methods of the Crusades against the Muslims. In July 1209 the Crusaders attacked Beziers, France, and killed Catholic and Cathar alike. This brutal—and indiscriminate—assault was recorded by Guilhem of Tudela, a cleric and troubadour (poet-musician) in his "Song of the Albigensian Crusade":

And so they made an exemplary carnage out of Beziers.
Not a soul survived. Who could say it better?
Who could say it worse?
The church? A slaughter-house.
The blood soaked the frescoes on the walls.
The Cross did not stop the ribald gang: priests, women,
infants, and old folks, all murdered. I'm telling you.

God receive their souls in his holy paradise!
I really believe that not since the Saracens
has the world known a more savage slaughter.

The brutal Albigensian Crusade lasted from 1209 to 1229. While it was still under way, Pope Gregory IX assumed the papal throne. He enlisted the services of the newly established Dominican Friars to preach the Crusade against the Albigenses in France and eventually throughout much of Europe. In addition, in 1233 he issued the first of several papal bulls (proclamations) calling for an "inquisition" (from the Latin *inquisitio,* investigation) of heretics. The Inquisition was to continue for several centuries. Throughout most of its history, it was guided by the principle that "error has no rights." While there had previously been some instances of heretics being burned at the stake, now such punishments enjoyed full papal support.

There were three major stages of the Inquisition: (1) the Medieval Inquisition of 1233 against heretics in France, Germany, and Italy (and by 1255 in all of central and western Europe); (2) the Spanish Inquisition of 1478 against Jews, Moors (Muslims), and Christian heretics in Spain (featuring the famed "Grand Inquisitor" Tomas de Torquemada) and in the 1500s in Mexico and Peru in the New World; and (3) the Roman Inquisition beginning in 1542 against Protestant heretics and Catholic dissidents in any jurisdiction of the Catholic faith. The Congregation of the Inquisition, called for most of its history the "Holy Office," was reorganized as the Congregation for the Doctrine of the Faith by Pope Paul VI in 1965.

These were the general procedures that were followed in inquisitions: (1) an inquisitor (priest) declared a thirty-day "grace period" to allow heretics to confess voluntarily; after that (2) a person accused of heresy was presumed to be guilty; (3) the accused was given the opportunity to confess and seek absolution; (4) the accused was brought before the inquisitor, questioned, and then tried; (5) the names of the accusers and witnesses against the accused were often withheld; (6) in the early years, legal representation and favorable witnesses were denied the accused (they were later permitted); (7) torture ("the rack") was permitted to obtain a confession and to secure the names of other heretics; and (8) upon confession or conviction of guilt, the heretic was sentenced at a public ceremony (called in Spain an *auto de fe*—"act of faith").

The most famous sentence meted out at an inquisition was death by burning at the stake. This punishment, however—as well as other punishments—were administered not by the church but rather by civil authority in order to protect clerics from having to "shed blood." Putting people to death at the stake was but one of many punishments that were meted out. Sentences ranged from the more draconian measures of death by drowning or hanging, exile, life imprisonment, or confiscation of property, to relatively benign punishments such as prayer, fasting, or pilgrimage. Sometimes people were "forgiven" merely for confessing or naming names. Sadism was not absent during the inquisitions; neither, however, was compassion.

Because there were few provisions to protect the innocent, the Inquisition was abused as spouse accused spouse, children betrayed parents, and political and economic enemies used the Inquisition to secure wealth and power for themselves. It is generally held, for example, that the charges against the Knights Templar were in fact false, but the Inquisition was an effective way to seize their considerable wealth and possessions. And what about torture? As time went on, it became evident that people will confess to anything and name anyone while "on the rack." Eventually the church abandoned these barbaric practices and people of the Middle Ages would be quite amazed to find that today the Catholic Church condemns the practice of capital punishment.

As we noted earlier, the initial target of the Inquisition was the Cathari (Albigenses) in southern France who, in addition to their heresy, were critical of the power and wealth of the Catholic clergy. As time went on, Jews too came to be considered targets of inquisitions, not only because they were "Christ killers" but also because they had become successful bankers and merchants. The Moors in Spain were also tried by the Inquisition for, of course, being infidels. Even non-Christian Gypsies (known today as "Romani") were subject to persecution. Indeed, there was almost no segment of the population—including clergy—that was immune from the Inquisition. Women, however, were to become its special victims.

Women with alleged magical powers were called witches (today the term "wicca" is used). We have a very early record of a witch trial that occurred in 1324 when Petronilla de Midia—maid of sorcerer Alice Kyteler—was burned at the stake in Kilkenny, Ireland. Women witches were special targets because they alone could give birth to demons who could destroy the church. (There were some men witches too, but women far outnumbered them). In addition, women were held to have magical powers over the earth and animals, over pain and disease, over the weather and the seasons—as well as sexual power over men. The inquisitors interpreted these magical powers in the worst possible light: they came from the Devil. Even simple fortunetellers were condemned.

The publication of the witch-hunters' manual *Malleus Malefi-carum* ("The Hammer of Witchcraft") in 1487 did much to stimulate persecution of women as witches. The manual details the nature of witchcraft and lists penances and punishments that include torture and death. Far more women than men were convicted of witchcraft because, in the words of the manual, women are "more fickle, weaker, stupider, and more lustful" than men.

Three years before the publication of *Malleus Maleficarum,* Pope Innocent VIII (pope from 1482 to 1492) issued a papal bull en-titled *Summis Desiderantes* ("With the Highest Desires") describing the "heretical depravity" of witches:

> ... many persons of both sexes, heedless of their own salva-tion and forsaking the Catholic faith, give themselves over to devils male and female, and by their incantations, charms, and conjurings, and by other abominable superstitions and sortileges, offences, crimes, and misdeeds, ruin and cause to perish the offspring of women, the foal of animals, the prod-ucts of the earth, the grapes of vines, and the fruits of trees, as well as men and women, cattle and flocks and herds and animals of every kind, vineyards also and orchards, mead-ows, pastures, harvests, grains and other fruits of the earth; they afflict and torture with dire pains and anguish, both in-ternal and external, these men, women, cattle, flocks, herds, and animals, and hinder men from begetting and women from conceiving, and prevent all consummation of marriage; moreover, they deny with sacrilegious lips the faith they re-ceived in holy Baptism; and, at the instigation of the enemy of mankind, they do not fear to commit and perpetuate many other abominable offences and crimes, at the risk of their own souls, to the insult of the Divine majesty, and to the per-nicious example and scandal of multitudes.

During the sixteenth and seventeenth centuries many women (and some men) were sentenced to death and more were imprisoned and tortured by the Catholic inquisitors and, after 1517, by Protestants as well. Heresy trials and witch-hunts continued in the Puritan colonies of North America and inquisitions were carried out in Central and South America too. Total war had not only gripped Europe but had also spread to the New World, to the native peoples of the newly "discovered" lands.

The Conquistadors: Crusades Abroad

While the Crusades against the Muslims were not military successes, they brought great wealth to merchants, traders, and seafarers. Genoa was one of the seafaring Italian cities that benefited most from the new trade that embraced Asia Minor, the Middle East, and North Africa as a result of the Crusades. Christopher Columbus (1451–1506), a Genoese sailor and explorer, was one of many at that time who sought a route by sea to the fabled riches of the East.

Columbus was heavily influenced by the apocalyptic ("second coming of Christ") preaching of Antonio de Marchena, who believed that the "heathen" had to be converted to Christ and the holy places recovered in Palestine before Christ could come again. In 1492 the Moors were conquered by the Spanish crown at Alhambra, and in that same year the Jews were expelled from Spain as part of the Spanish Inquisition. Columbus seized upon these victories to persuade King Ferdinand and Queen Isabella to fund a "westerly route" to secure riches from the East so that Spain could "spend all the profits of this...enterprise on the conquest of Jerusalem."

The Spanish crown had little to lose and a great deal to gain from such a proposal. If Columbus were to be successful, Spain could claim exclusive glory for what the English, French, Germans, and Italians had failed to do: conquer Jerusalem forever from the "infidels." Columbus believed that the prospect of mounting a final Crusade against the Muslims was decisive in his negotiations with the Spanish court.

Columbus was convinced that God had made him "the messenger of the new heaven and the new earth." And so, with the Crusader cross emblazoned on the sails of his ships, and with the conviction that he had been sent by God, Columbus accidentally discovered what he thought were the outer islands of China. Despite the known presence of people on the islands—who welcomed Columbus warmly—Columbus relates: "The Admiral went on shore in the armed boat . . . bore the royal standard . . . and took possession of that island for the King and Queen" of Spain. The Crusades had arrived in the New World.

In reality, Christian Europe in the person of Columbus did not "discover" a "new world"; it *invaded* an *old* one. During his four voyages to the Caribbean, Columbus enslaved the Indians and robbed them of their gold and silver. When there was little gold to be had, he and the Conquistadors ("Conquerors") who followed him set up large agricultural *encomiendas* (estates) where enslaved Indians would bring agricultural goods and other forms of wealth to be sent back to Spain. Just as the Crusaders had toward the Saracens, the Conquistadors undertook their mission "in God's name, for God's glory, and for God's gain."

In time the conquered people of the Americas came to see the Crusader cross in much the way as the Muslims did: as a symbol of violence and conquest. A native of what is now Nicaragua, for example, asked: "What is a Christian, what are Christians? They ask for maize, for honey, for cotton, for women, for gold, for silver; Christians will not work, they are liars, gamblers, perverse, and they swear." Even some of the earliest Indians who resisted the Christian invasion were burned at the stake, hanged, and tortured in inquisitorial fashion. Many committed suicide and ceased having babies rather than cooperate with the Conquistadors.

As the Conquistadors such as Hernan Cortez (who captured Mexico in 1522–1524), Francisco Pizarro (who conquered Peru in 1533), and Hernando De Soto (who exploited the Indians in the North American southeast in the 1530s) spread throughout Central and South America, they brought with them not only war but also smallpox, measles, typhus, and other diseases that would kill millions of Indians. Even in Columbus's own lifetime, this "necessitated" the importation of slaves from Africa to replace the vanished Indians, especially in the Caribbean. The fortunes in gold and silver that were made enriched first the Spanish aristocracy, then the Portuguese, and then the English, the French, the Dutch, etc. But none of this wealth went to a new Crusade to recapture Jerusalem.

A similar pattern emerged in North America. The Puritans, who had emigrated from England, believed they had come to found a "New Jerusalem," a "city on a hill" that was to be a "light to all nations." There was, however, no room for the Indians who inhabited the land God had "given" to the Puritans. Like the Conquistadors, the colonists either killed the Indians or exploited them through treaties that were to be broken again and again. In words reminiscent of the language used for the Saracens, Indians were referred to as "a treacherous and barbarous enemy," and of course, repeatedly degraded as "savages." In addition to persecuting the Indians of North America, religious leaders engaged in witch trials against women, and they tortured and hanged even pacifist Quakers. Finally, like the Conquistadors, the European colonists imported African slaves to build their new empire.

To sum up: There were, in reality, scores of wars, persecutions, and colonial expansionist movements that were either called "Crusades" or were inspired by them. There is no question that the Crusades had a far-reaching impact on the Muslim world, on Europe, and on the Americas—and, as we shall see, that impact continues into our own day.

The Fascist Security State

No discussion of total war as "war without end" would be complete without a brief examination of fascism. Although the term "fascism" was coined in the twentieth century, the central belief in "superior" and "inferior" human beings or in "freemen" and "slaves" has existed in many cultures, ancient and contemporary. Both Plato and Aristotle, for example, thought the world was divided into "free" and "slave." Many philosophers including Nicolo Machiavelli (1469–1528), Thomas Hobbes (1588–1679), Arthur Schopenhauer (1788–1860), and Friedrich Nietzsche (1844–1900) believed that the only language the masses could understand was one of power and control.

Fascism is a totalitarian political philosophy that holds that national corporate survival rests on perpetual warfare with enemies both foreign (other nations) and domestic (dissident political groups). Benito Mussolini (1883–1945), who first used the word "fascist," believed that Italy's economic and cultural problems could be solved only by supreme state power wielded by one political party that was headed by a charismatic leader (such as "Il Duce" in Italy or "Der Fuhrer" in Germany).

The twentieth century saw the rise of a number of fascist governments, not only in Italy and Germany but also in Japan, Austria, Spain, and Portugal. Although Communist societies differ in important ways from fascist states, they have also exhibited fascist tendencies.

Following are some of the key characteristics of fascist philosophy:

National supremacy. Fascists believe their nation to be superior to all others. They see it as having a mission that is unique in human history. Because their nation is unique, they are not bound by international law, or treaties, or alliances. The nation's mission is not to *cooperate* with others but rather to *dominate* or control them. Appeals to the "past" are useless, since a new and glorious history mandates the state to create an international order that is unprecedented, and that it alone controls.

Perpetual war. War is a normal and desirable manner of pursuing national political interests. Every generation must receive mandatory military training and be tested in battle to keep the nation strong and vigilant. War is also a means of securing needed resources and wealth, and of dominating lesser nations. Negotiation and compromise signal weakness; generals must wage "aggressive wars." National leaders are strongest when the state is continually at war.

One political party. The only political party with legitimacy is the one that controls the government, the courts, the economy, the press, art and literature, and even sports. Democracy is regarded as "collective decadence," since only the elite (Nietzsche's "superman") understand what is good for the people. The party leader who rules the nation must exhibit virility and firmness in dealing with the country's enemies. In order to remain strong, even the ruling political party must periodically be purged of dissident or mediocre members.

Virility and violence. Just as nations achieve superiority through war, men achieve manhood through combat. Fascists believe that femininity leads to weakness and degradation, and only masculinity expressed as "virility" can build a strong society. Every generation of men must be "purified" by battle. Some fascists have been inspired by the "virile warrior Christianity of the Crusades." Women should be obedient wives; their role is to bear many children for the state.

Racial scapegoating. Only those who are "racially pure" may participate in the affairs of state. Consequently, the state must "purge" itself of those who would dilute and weaken the nation. While most fascist countries persecuted Jews, other groups that were attacked included Gypsies, homosexuals, members of trade unions, immigrants, artists, intellectuals, feminists, pacifists, liberals, and Communists. Victories belong to the "master race"; mistakes and failures are caused by the subversive activity of "impure vermin." The fascist state is infallible; therefore, disloyal ethnic or philosophical minorities are responsible for error and must be publicly condemned and persecuted.

Education for power. Education exists to serve the needs of the state and to create a culture of submission and obedience among the people. Teachers who do not serve the cultural and political interests of the state are to be fired or imprisoned. Intellectuals who think independently are subversive and are to be ridiculed as "elite snobs." Education must build the character of the young citizens and not waste their time with useless intellectual speculation or idle dreaming. Since the state defines "reality," the social sciences and those disciplines that rely on empirical, objective data are ridiculed, banned, or distorted.

State capitalism. The state as a "corporate" entity encourages the upper economic classes to produce wealth for the state. Independent labor unions and socialist consumer collectives are banned as counterproductive and subversive. Fascism strongly supports the capitalist philosophy of profit without restrictions, since great wealth is needed to support perpetual war. The state must rely heavily on wealthy private corporations to arm, feed, and even fight the nation's wars.

Control of the media and art. In a fascist society, every news story, every song, every concert, every poem, every essay is a "political" act that must serve the state. Journalists and artists who hold that "truth" and "beauty" transcend the state are to be silenced or disciplined. "Free" speech and "free" artistic expression are permitted only if they serve the interests of the state. Graphic artists are to produce posters and other displays that promote loyalty and patriotism. Films should glorify the ruling elite.

Police state. "Human rights" are *privileges* that are granted by the state and, therefore, may be denied by the state. Consequently, police and security forces must control abuses of freedom of the press, of association, of free speech, and of religion that are granted by the state. Every citizen is under continual surveillance; family members, friends, and neighbors are required to report on those they even suspect of violating the laws or interfering with the good order of the state. There is no obligation to provide accused people with legal protections, since "error has no rights." An independent judiciary cannot be permitted, because a nation's laws must serve the interests of the state.

State religion. The state must replace the decadent religions of the past with its own spiritual identity, national rituals, and ethical system. Some fascist states recall the glories of their "pagan" past or model themselves on the Greek Spartan military state. Traditional religions like Christianity or Buddhism can be co-opted into state service through "guarantees" that their property and buildings will be exempt from taxes and that they will have freedom of worship as long as they are silent on political matters. Authentic religion is worship of the state.

In a fascist state there is nothing higher than "politics," not even ethics. Hence the twin ethical principles of fascism are "might makes right" and "the end justifies the means." Accordingly, the "good" result of an all-powerful state may be achieved by any means, including actions that are normally held to be unethical. This explains how fascists rise to power and maintain power: by lying to the people. Since fascism generally blossoms during times of emergency such as economic depression, or war, or terrorist attack, fascists seize upon these opportunities to deny civil liberties, or to steal elections, or to assassinate the character of political opponents. Fear and ignorance are the greatest allies of the fascist.

In this discussion we have been focusing on twentieth-century examples of fascist states. However, fascism continues to have its advocates today, and its expression is not limited to governments. Fascist movements have appeared in such diverse countries as France, Belgium, Greece, Norway, South Africa, Chile, Brazil, China, Mexico, and the United States. Fascist tendencies can be found in such organizations as the Ku Klux Klan, the neo-Nazi skinheads, and other white supremacist organizations. Fascist tendencies can even be found in mainstream political parties and religions.

Terrorism and Total War

The terrorist attacks of September 11, 2001, on the United States caused an immediate reaction on the part of total war advocates. They claimed that they alone could adequately respond to the attacks because they understood the principles upon which the terrorist actions were based. Further, they stated that they knew best how to respond: with even greater force against the attackers.

A total war response to terrorism endorses:

- *Preventive war.* The best long-term solution to terrorist action is to wage war against a terrorist stronghold, or host nation, or rogue state while plans are still being *contemplated* for an attack on the United States (or another state). As soon as the "intention" to engage in terrorist or military behavior is evident, there is a duty to wage war against the terrorists so as to prevent them from proceeding any further. One should not wait until terrorists or rogue nations have the weapons or means necessary to launch terrorist attacks. International organizations such as the United Nations should not be relied upon, since diplomatic efforts may only provide the enemy with more time to prepare an attack.

- *Preemptive strikes.* Assassinations and covert military attacks against suspected terrorist individuals or groups should precede or accompany preventive war. Special operations ("special ops") counterterrorist forces such as the Delta Force and the British Special Air Service (SAS) should be inserted into terrorist locations to "surgically" remove terrorists or potential terrorists. In addition, organizations such as the Central Intelligence Agency (CIA) should recruit spies and agents to destabilize terrorist organizations from within. Privatized military personnel—mercenaries—should be employed by governments to attack terrorists, especially when governmental leaders want to deny responsibility for military action on foreign soil.

- *Retaliatory strikes.* After a terrorist act, the nation attacked should immediately respond with land, sea, and air attacks that retaliate in a massive way for the damage that was done to them. Innocent civilians will of course be killed in such attacks ("collateral damage"), but the responsibility for their deaths lies with the terrorists, not with the nation that was attacked. Military strikes should be conducted against nations that harbor terrorist groups. Prisoners are to be treated as criminals; isolation and torture are acceptable punishments.

- *Global dominance.* A nation cannot be truly free from terrorist attack while it remains subservient to, or in alliance with, other nation states. Authentic security can be achieved only when a nation is the sole "mega-power" that dominates and controls other nations. The mega-power should have an international police and spy network that will immediately signal any terrorist threat around the world. Nations that seek military parity with the mega-power are to be considered *de facto* enemies who may be subject to preventive war and preemptive military strikes. There can be no peace until other nations adopt political systems that support the mega-power.

Although terrorism on the scale that we have known it in the twenty-first century is new, the total war response is not new. Its rationale has roots in the perspectives that gave rise to the medieval Crusades and to subsequent wars, persecutions, and movements inspired by the Crusades. Some of the assumptions common to both the Crusades (and the Inquisition, the wars of conquest in the Ameri-

cas, and even fascism) and a total war response to terrorism include
the following:

- Might makes right.
- Error has no rights.
- The end justifies the means.
- Enemies must be annihilated.
- In a time of war there is no clear distinction between
    legitimate and illegitimate behavior.
- War abroad demands unity at home.

It is worth noting that the similarities are not limited to obvious
common assumptions. The Crusades and Crusade-inspired movements were grounded in a sense of divine "righteousness," and their
stated aims had to do with noble ideals, such as justice and truth and
liberation. The same could be said of today's total war response to
terrorism. However, as in the case of the Crusades and the movements they inspired, total war also has political and economic dimensions which, while perhaps unstated, are certainly operative.

Conclusion

Thus concludes our discussion of total war in Christian history.
As we have seen, total wars were holy wars that were originally
fought against Muslims, and then against other Christians, Jews,
witches, and Indians. Though the fascist security state has clear
"pagan" roots, it also was influenced by the Crusades and was certainly supported with a good deal of fervor by some Christians, both
Catholic and Protestant.

Although no "mainstream" Catholic or Protestant churches (those
who belong, for example, to the World Council of Churches) teach
total war, millions of fundamentalist and evangelical Christians (most
belong to independent Christian churches) believe that a "cosmic
war" that will destroy the world and usher in the triumphant kingdom
of God is imminent. Some Christians believe that the "end times" are
already upon us and that a cataclysmic "total" war *must* take place
before Christ can reign again.

Historically, many fundamentalist leaders and churches have been militant anti-Communists who have vigorously supported American military intervention abroad along with high U.S. defense spending. Indeed, some fundamentalists assert that the United States is "the" instrument of God's salvation for the world and, hence, that the United States has a duty to wage war for peace.

Not all fundamentalist or evangelical Christians, however, endorse militarist policies. Christian groups such as Evangelicals for Social Action (ESA) and Sojourners as well as like-minded members of the historic peace churches (Mennonites, Brethren, Quakers) are strongly oriented toward pacifism in their response to war. There are also mainstream evangelical Catholics and Protestants who stand with ESA and Sojourners.

Historian Roland Bainton has stated, "Wars are more humane when God is left out of them." When wars are fought in God's name they are more vicious and indiscriminate than wars that are fought for national defense or even for territorial gain. Killing in God's name frees us from the moral responsibility that is ours if we kill solely for our own purposes. Killing in God's name permits us to rejoice that we are called to be "Christian soldiers" who would establish God's reign of peace on earth. Unlike the just war model, which calls for war to be undertaken with a "mournful" attitude, the total war model celebrates war as a divine mandate.

The Total War Model: A Summary

The following are key points that characterize the total war model:

1. Human beings are naturally aggressive and warlike. The tendency to injure and kill, the proclivity to attack people and seize their territory, and the desire to engage in violent combat are "instincts" or innate characteristics of the human species. There is a biological link between violence and virility, and boys become men through military service and combat. Only the fittest survive.

2. Human society is in a perpetual state of war. Since human beings are naturally violent, it follows logically that the societies they create will always be characterized by strife and violent conflict. The societies that survive will be those most militarily prepared to fight enemies, both foreign and domestic. Societies at war cannot tolerate a free press or an independent judiciary, since they weaken the war effort.

3. Warriors are moral exemplars and national heroes. A nation's highest praise and status are accorded to soldiers who defend the nation through the extermination of its enemies. Children in a nation's schools are taught to hold military leaders in the highest esteem and are educated to serve in the military themselves at the proper age. Pictures and statues of a nation's warriors appear in schools, in concert halls, and in public parks.

4. Preventive wars and preemptive military strikes are morally legitimate. To protect the nation, leaders must presume that other nations are preparing to attack. A leader has a duty, therefore, to attack another nation while it is still *contemplating* an attack on his own nation. Any nation that possesses weapons is a potential enemy. To wait for an *actual* attack is to shirk one's duty to defend the public. War is always a *first* resort in a potential crisis. It is better to attack first than to be sorry later for having failed to do so.

5. The goal of war is victory that results in unconditional surrender. Since there are only "good guys" and "bad guys" in any war, it is the obligation of the righteous nation to utterly destroy the actually or potentially offending nation. To allow "conditions" for surrender is to permit evil to continue to exist; victory demands total and complete surrender. Before war begins, international institutions and other nations must be prohibited from attempting to resolve the dispute, since that will only give the enemy more time to prepare for an attack.

6. The killing of civilians is morally acceptable. Armies can exist only if they are supported by the taxes and moral support of a nation's civilian population. Children are potential soldiers, and the children in an enemy country will grow up to be enemies. Hence, they are legitimate targets. Factory workers, teachers, farmers, and business people all support war and, therefore, are *de facto* combatants.

7. Nuclear, biological, and chemical (NBC) weapons of mass destruction (WMD) may be used in war. In addition to the large-scale use of conventional military weapons, a nation may use NBC weapons even if they result in casualties at home. The preemptive use of NBC weapons (or space-based laser weapons) will bring a swift conclusion to a conflict, thus saving the lives of millions of civilians and soldiers. Even the threat to use weapons like these can save many lives. International treaties that ban the use of such weapons should be ignored in the interest of effective political and military policy.

8. Civilian and military commanders can expect unquestioning obedience from their citizens and soldiers. Total war cannot be successfully waged without the absolute obedience of those who are called upon to support or fight in it. Since dissent provides "aid and comfort to the enemy" and weakens the morale of the troops in combat, dissidents should be silenced or jailed. In time of war it is acceptable to abrogate the rights of opposition political parties and to suspend individual civil rights.

9. A national security state is essential. A national security state should be established that has a permanent military draft and an integrated military/industrial/research complex for the development of new weapons systems. The state must have unlimited police and judicial power to defend against enemies, domestic and foreign. Peace and harmony can exist in a country only when it has a large, experienced combat force that is supported by the best weapons available. Children should study military science in order to prepare them for eventual military service. All economic, social, religious, and judicial institutions have a political mission: to provide security for the state.

10. True peace requires a global empire. It is the goal of the national security state to become a "mega-power" or global empire so that true peace may exist on earth. The long-range goal of such a state is to bring peace on earth through domination of the almost two hundred nation states that presently exist in the world. In order to minimize dissent and violence, the global empire must fashion a world culture that is based on the dominant state's social, economic, political, and religious system. The global empire must establish the rule of law so that order may characterize human relations.

———————— • ————————

It's time to write another letter to Nicole to assist her in understanding the philosophy of total war. In your letter, please answer the following questions:

1. What is the biblical basis for total war?

2. Why did Christianity launch the Crusades?

3. How did the Crusades continue in Christian history?

4. What is the total war response to terrorism?

5. What, in your view, are the three most important key points in the total war model?

After answering these questions, please state your own views on total war. What are its strong points? Its weak points?

This information will help Nicole as she integrates an understanding of total war with what she has learned about just war and pacifism.

Recommended Reading

The following books are recommended if you would like to learn more about total war:

Hannah Arendt. *The Origins of Totalitarianism*. Harcourt, Inc., A Harvest Book, 1994

Karen Armstrong. *Holy War: The Crusades and Their Impact on Today's World*. Anchor Books, 2001.

James Turner Johnson. *The Holy War Idea in Western and Islamic Traditions*. Pennsylvania State University Press, 2001.

Tomaz Mastnak. *Crusading Peace: Christendom, the Muslim World, and Western Political Order*. University of California Press, 2002.

Jonathan Riley-Smith, ed. *The Oxford Illustrated History of the Crusades*. Oxford University Press, 1995.

Ludwig von Mises. *Omnipotent Government: The Rise of the Total State and Total War*. Libertarian Press, 1985.

World Community

"Nothing could be worse than the fear that one had given up too soon and left one unexpended effort which might have saved the world."
Jane Addams

Introduction

World Community is a social philosophy that advocates the creation of an international democratic union of states that will abolish war, defend human rights, secure social justice, and protect the environment for future generations.

Advocates of World Community believe this level of global governance is evolving from present village, city, nation, and international unions and alliances. World Community will be distinguished by the rule of international law that secures justice for all and guarantees human rights through a world charter that includes a bill of rights to protect political minorities from the tyranny of the majority.

World Community rejects the flawed biological notion that there are distinct "races" of the single biological species *homo sapiens*. All human beings share the same biological and psychological makeup, the same economic desires and political needs, and the same social and spiritual destiny. Because of this "natural" unity of humankind, advocates of World Community hold that it is merely a matter of time before a global political and economic agency will be created to address the commonality of human needs. There is only *one* race: the human race.

The period of the "high nation state" ended as humankind entered the twenty-first century of the Common Era. The sovereign nation state is rapidly becoming obsolete in the face of international environmental, economic, and social problems that can be effectively addressed only by a level of governance that is competent to solve these truly *inter*national problems. World Community will not, however, replace or eliminate local forms of governance that have proven to be effective in solving *intra*national problems.

World Community advocates include those who support global governance from a "principled" perspective, and those who accept it as a "pragmatic" necessity. "Principled" advocates of World Community contend that humankind has a duty to recognize the spiritual unity of human beings through the establishment of a global union that promotes the rights of humans and other species through international law.

"Pragmatic" advocates of World Community adopt a more "consequentialist" approach, which holds that global union is simply a more efficient or cost-effective way to solve problems that cannot be handled at the national level. In addition, some pragmatists believe that military force will still be necessary in a global union of states. "Principled" and "pragmatic" advocates of World Community both agree, however, that the nation state is obsolete and that one of its greatest legacies, war, can and must be abolished.

It is important to note that, unlike pacifism, just war, and total war, World Community has existed in history only as an ideal. Therefore, we need to approach this model with a considerable degree of intellectual humility. Critics contend that it is unrealistic and even dangerous to assert that a "global union" can end war. But World Community advocates hold that many great ideas were rejected when they were first proposed. With Victor Hugo, they contend that "an invasion of armies can be resisted, but not an idea whose time has come."

Although we are unaware of it, we may be living in as dramatic a time as the first century when Christian pacifism was first introduced, or the fifth century when the just war entered Christian history, or the twelfth century when total war became the norm. Many years from now historians may look back and state, "Although they didn't know it then, the citizens of the twenty-first century began the dramatic process that resulted in a global union that abolished war and secured social justice for all."

World Community advocates are inspired by the words of John Lennon:

Imagine all the people, living life in peace.
You may say I'm a dreamer, but I'm not the only one.
I hope someday you'll join us, and the world will be as one.

We turn, now, to a discussion of World Community in the Hebrew and Christian Scriptures.

World Community in the Hebrew Scriptures

The Bible is the story of the relationship between the Jewish people and their God. It is a story rooted very much in the history of the
Jewish people's repeated attempts to establish and maintain a national
homeland. Consequently, there are many stories of wars and struggles
between the Jewish people and other "wandering" people of the desert
over who owned land that each called "home." Today's division in the
Middle East between Jew (Israel) and Arab (Palestine) is a microcosm
of a very long history that has troubled that multi-ethnic region.

The contemporary problem of exactly who owns the "Holy Land"
is complicated by the historical fact that Jews, Christians, and Muslims have all—at one time or another in their histories—claimed that
the land in question was given to them by God. Further complicating
the situation is the fact that Jews, Christians, and Muslims all pray to
the *same* God. Consequently, the struggle for land in the Middle East
is as much a theological debate as it is a political one. Whose side is
God on?

Advocates of World Community contend that God is on *all* sides
in this struggle. "Look at the Bible," they say. The book of Genesis
records: "So God created humankind in his image, in the image of
God he created them; male and female he created them" (Genesis
1:27). Genesis does *not* state that God created "Jewish," or "Muslim,"
or "Buddhist," or "Russian," or "American," or "Korean" human beings. "Humankind" includes all these religious and ethnic groups and
many more. God's creation of humankind was an inclusive act that ex-
cluded no one.

In the chapter on pacifism we reviewed several passages from
the Hebrew Scriptures that pacifists use to demonstrate the Jewish
tradition of nonviolence. Like pacifists, World Community advocates find inspiration in the Hebrew prophets. Particularly notewor-

thy is the prophet Isaiah. World Community advocates especially like to quote this passage:

> In days to come
>> the mountain of the LORD's house
> shall be established as the highest of the mountains,
>> and shall be raised above the hills;
> all the nations shall stream to it.
> Many peoples shall come and say,
> "Come, let us go up to the mountain of the LORD,
>> to the house of the God of Jacob;
> that he may teach us his ways
>> and that we may walk in his paths."
> For out of Zion shall go forth instruction,
>> and the word of the LORD from Jerusalem.
> He shall judge between the nations,
>> and shall arbitrate for many peoples;
> they shall beat their swords into ploughshares,
>> and their spears into pruning-hooks;
> nation shall not lift up sword against nation,
>> neither shall they learn war any more.
>> (Isaiah 2:2–4)

World Community advocates who are inspired by a vision of faith hold that this passage highlights the inevitable unity of all humankind under the protection of God. They contend that war is created by humans, not by God, and that if people follow God's "ways," war will be abolished on earth. Humanists are inspired by a vision of humankind that uses arbitration rather than war to settle disputes and that converts military spending into food production.

The Hebrew Scriptures strongly advocate a peace that is based on justice. The Jewish people are repeatedly told that, rather than relying on "chariots" or armies, they are to rely on God even for success in battle. But authentic peace rests on the work of justice. Isaiah looks to a day when God's "servant" produces peace on earth through the work of justice:

> Here is my servant, whom I uphold,
>> my chosen, in whom my soul delights;

I have put my spirit upon him;
>   he will bring forth justice to the nations.
He will not cry or lift up his voice,
>   or make it heard in the street;
a bruised reed he will not break,
>   and a dimly burning wick he will not quench;
>   he will faithfully bring forth justice.
He will not grow faint or be crushed
>   until he has established justice in the earth;
>   and the coastlands wait for his teaching.

Thus says God, the LORD,
>   who created the heavens and stretched them out,
>   who spread out the earth and what comes from it,
who gives breath to the people upon it
>   and spirit to those who walk in it:
I am the LORD, I have called you in righteousness,
>   I have taken you by the hand and kept you;
I have given you as a covenant to the people,
>   a light to the nations,
>   to open the eyes that are blind,
to bring out the prisoners from the dungeon,
>   from the prison those who sit in darkness.
>   (Isaiah 42:1–7)

World Community advocates believe this passage highlights the necessity for global justice as the only secure foundation for international peace. They contend that the Lord's call to "righteousness" applies not just to Jews, but to all creatures of God. This positive theme is continued in the Christian Scriptures.

World Community in the Christian Scriptures

Jesus preached a message of universal salvation that was based on the call of the Hebrew prophets to justice. In describing his mission, Jesus directly quoted from the prophet Isaiah:

"The Spirit of the Lord is upon me,
>   because he has anointed me to bring good news to the poor.

He has sent me to proclaim release to the captives
    and recovery of sight to the blind,
    to let the oppressed go free,
to proclaim the year of the Lord's favor." (Luke 4:18–19)

While Jesus spoke these words to people who were victims of the Roman occupation forces in Palestine, World Community advocates hold that the message has universal appeal in that it refers to liberation on a global scale. Christianity is at heart a missionary religion with an international orientation. In the last words in the Gospel of Matthew, Jesus tells his disciples,

> "Go therefore and make disciples of all nations, baptizing them in the name of the Father and of the Son and of the Holy Spirit, and teaching them to obey everything that I have commanded you. And remember, I am with you always, to the end of the age." (Matthew 28:19–20)

We do well to recall that in his ministry Jesus constantly violated religious laws that forbade him from talking to sinners or non-Jews (especially Samaritans). Scripture scholars tell us that Jesus' command to make disciples "of all nations" means that the gospel was not meant exclusively for Jewish people and was properly oriented toward all religions and ethnic groups.

The numerous letters of the early Christian writer Paul focus strongly on the cosmic peace that results from the death and resurrection of Jesus. In Paul's view, Jesus' death has created a new humanity, a "new self" that replaces the violent and selfish human being of old. This "new self" transcends national, economic, or gender differences. Paul relates:

> As many of you as were baptized into Christ have clothed yourselves with Christ. There is no longer Jew or Greek, there is no longer slave or free, there is no longer male and female; for all of you are one in Christ Jesus. And if you belong to Christ, then you are Abraham's offspring, heirs according to the promise. (Galatians 3:27–29)

In his letter to the Colossians, Paul phrases his thought in a slightly different way, "... there is no longer Greek and Jew, circumcised and uncircumcised, barbarian, Scythian, slave and free; but Christ is all and in all" (Colossians 3:11).

In these passages, Paul is pointing to the spiritual unity of humankind and to the cosmic salvation that Christ's death accomplished for all people. Salvation is universal because the barriers that separated humankind were torn asunder by the life and death of Jesus. Paul is called the "Apostle to the Gentiles" precisely because he recognized the universal mission of the gospel message to free all humankind from religious and ethnic idolatry. For Paul, Christ was truly "all and in all."

Above all, Paul believed that Jesus had freed all people from slavish obedience to the letter of the law. Mere obedience to any law (including the Jewish law) was, in his opinion, no guarantee of either civilization or salvation. Above all, Paul insisted that "doers" of the law were superior to mere "hearers" of the law. In addition, all humans (including those who were "Gentiles" or non-Jews) would be judged by God on how well they had followed the law "written on their hearts." He tells us,

> For it is not the hearers of the law who are righteous in God's sight, but the doers of the law who will be justified [saved]. When Gentiles, who do not possess the law, do instinctively what the law requires, these, though not having the law, are a law to themselves. They show that what the law requires is written on their hearts, to which their own conscience also bears witness; and their conflicting thoughts will accuse or perhaps excuse them on the day when, according to my gospel, God, through Jesus Christ, will judge the secret thoughts of all. (Romans 1:13–16)

The reference in this passage to non-Jews (Gentiles) who "do instinctively what the law requires" tells us that Paul thought God's moral law was written into human nature. People will be judged by how well they follow the law "written on their hearts" that is found in "their own conscience."

And how are the "doers of the law" to behave? Paul called upon the Christians as "one body in Christ" to renew and transform themselves and the social order. In the following passage, Paul presents a blueprint for international peace:

Let love be genuine; hate what is evil, hold fast to what is good; love one another with mutual affection; outdo one another in showing honor. Do not lag in zeal, be ardent in spirit, serve the Lord. Rejoice in hope, be patient is suffering, persevere in prayer. Contribute to the needs of the saints; extend hospitality to strangers.

Bless those who persecute you; bless and do not curse them. Rejoice with those who rejoice, weep with those who weep. Live in harmony with one another; do not be haughty, but associate with the lowly; do not claim to be wiser than you are. Do not repay anyone evil for evil, but take thought for what is noble in the sight of all. If it is possible, so far as it depends on you, live peaceably with all.

Beloved, never avenge yourselves, but leave room for the wrath of God; for it is written, "Vengeance is mine, I will repay, says the Lord." No, "if your enemies are hungry, feed them; if they are thirsty, give them something to drink; for by doing this you will heap burning coals on their heads." Do not be overcome by evil, but overcome evil with good. (Romans 12:9–21)

These are lofty and difficult sentiments. Paul is challenging his readers to rise above the assumptions of the culture of hatred, revenge, and war. Can love of enemies work in the real world? Will rebuilding the hospitals, schools, and homes of those who attack us make them stop hating us? Are forgiveness and reconciliation really the way out of our present madness? Can love be a social force in international relations?

History tells us that the Christian churches have answered these questions with something less than success. Many individuals and small Christian communities have, however, successfully labored for peace through justice, even at the international level. World Community advocates contend that "love" is a spiritual force that can be more effective than war in securing a peace based on justice.

The following perspectives on World Community are found in the Hebrew and Christian Scriptures:

- All human beings are created in the image of God.
- War will be abolished when people follow God's path.

- Peace between nations is based on the work of justice.
- A common humanity transcends all ethnic and religious
     differences.
- God's law is written into the heart of every human being.

Natural Law

The apostle Paul's belief that God's "eternal" law is written into human nature and that it can be discovered through reason is foundational to a Christian philosophy of international relations. This "natural law" endows every human being—baptized or not—with the ability to know and carry out the divine will through human action. Indeed, the law of nature is the foundation of human rights and the basis of all laws that are made by legislative bodies.

But the concept of natural law did not originate with the Christian religion. The notion that human reason is the source of ethical behavior can be found in the thought of Plato and Aristotle in Greece and Seneca and Cicero in Rome, as well as in the philosophy of the Cynics and the Stoics. The ancient Romans had a concept of international law called "the law of nations" *(ius gentium)* that recognized that "aliens" or non-citizens of Rome were nevertheless entitled to the same rights as Romans by virtue of their common humanity. Ancient philosophers essentially held that rights and justice flowed from human nature itself (natural law), rather than merely from laws made by governments (positive law).

The principal philosophical advocates of "natural law" were the Stoics (members of a school of philosophy founded by Zeno around 300 BCE), who believed that all persons shared a common human nature and that people of all nations could live in harmony and peace with each other. Stoics saw themselves as "citizens of the world," bound, in Cicero's words, by "one eternal and unchangeable law" that "will be valid for all nations and for all times."

The Stoic Roman emperor Marcus Aurelius (121–180 CE; emperor from 161 to 180) summed up a good deal of Stoic philosophy in this selection from his *Meditations*:

Constantly regard the universe as one living being, having one substance and one soul; and observe how all things have reference to one perception, the perception of this one living being; and how all things act with one movement; and how all things are the cooperating causes of all things which exist; observe too the continuous spinning of the thread and the contexture of the web. (4.40)

The biblical theology of creation, the philosophy of Aristotle and of the Stoics, and the teaching of the Jewish philosopher Moses Maimonides (1135–1204 CE) contributed to the thought of Dominican theologian Thomas Aquinas (1225–1274) on natural law. Writing in the *Summa Theologica*, Aquinas taught that "natural law is nothing else than the rational creature's participation in the eternal law." Further, Aquinas believed that "in man there is first of all an inclination to do good in accordance with the nature which he has in common with all substances." Essentially, Aquinas taught that all created things are good because God who is perfectly good cannot create anything that is evil.

Aquinas taught that the natural law included the following concepts: (1) all human beings have an inclination to the good; (2) the good promotes security and survival; (3) sexual intercourse and the education of children are natural to humans; (4) people have an inclination to know God and to live in society (see I-II, Q. 94, Art. 2). Aquinas realized that while these concepts are universal, they are not known equally by all due to error, or vice, or cultural differences (hence the need for education). Nevertheless, he held that natural law "can nowise be blotted out from men's hearts."

The following perspectives on World Community can be found in the concept of natural law:

- Human beings can discover God's law through reason.
- Human beings have a natural inclination to preserve the species.
- A universal "law of nations" governs all human beings.
- Ignorance, culture, and vice can hinder natural law.

The teaching of Aquinas and his followers (known as the "scholastic" school) on natural law has had a profound effect on Catholic and humanistic teaching on peace and justice matters down to our own time. This was especially true in the great debate that took place in sixteenth-century Spain on whether the newly "discovered" Indians in the Americas were human beings, whether they were creatures of God who had souls. We turn now to that discussion.

Do Indians Have Souls?

If people from Earth were to travel to another planet and find life forms there, they might ask, "Who are these beings? Are they like us? Are they people?" This is exactly what happened with Columbus's "discovery" of an old world that Europeans called the "New World." Who or "what" were the native people that the Spaniards called "Indios" or Indians? Were they barbarians or human beings? Was their destiny to be sub-human slaves or free people? The answers to these questions were to set the stage for the development of the World Community model in Christian history.

When "Admiral of the Ocean Sea" Christopher Columbus landed on that mysterious island in the Caribbean in 1492, he unfurled the royal banner and took "possession of the island for the King and Queen" of Spain. He erected a cross "as a token of our Lord Jesus Christ" and named the island "San Salvador" ("Holy Savior"). Concerning the naked, virtually unarmed Indians who warmly welcomed him to their island, Columbus found them "friendly and well-dispositioned." Indeed, Columbus thought of them as "a people who can be made free and converted to our Holy Faith more by love than by force."

Only slowly would the trusting Taino Indians come to realize that Columbus and Imperial Spain had every intention of stealing their land and destroying their culture. Columbus's rhetoric about making the Indians "free" through "love" did not last long, since he also remarked that "they ought to make good and skilled servants [slaves]" and that "with fifty men [soldiers] you could subject everyone and make them do what you wished." Thus began a long "trail of tears" that would, in the centuries that followed, devastate the Indian peoples and cultures of what was to become North and South America.

From the very beginning there were bitter divisions on whether the Indians were people or whether they were to be enslaved as "barbarians." Certainly Columbus and his immediate followers treated them as slaves when they established agricultural *encomiendas* (plantations) where the Indians were forced to work for the Spaniards. An early voice opposing this exploitation was that of the Dominican friar Antonio de Montesinos, who in 1511 shocked the Spanish colonizers by calling for the freedom of the Indians and stating that those who enslaved them had no chance for salvation.

In his address to the assembled Spanish notables (including Admiral Diego Colon) on Hispaniola, Montesinos spoke for all the Dominican friars when he stated:

> "You are all in mortal sin! You live in it and you die in it! Why? Because of the cruelty and tyranny you use with these innocent people. Tell me, with what right, with what justice, do you hold these Indians in such cruel and horrible servitude [slavery]? On what authority have you waged such detestable wars on these people, in their mild, peaceful lands, where you have consumed such infinitudes of them, wreaking upon [them] this death and unheard of havoc? How is it that you hold them so crushed and exhausted, giving them nothing to eat, nor any treatment for their diseases, which you cause them to be infected with through the surfeit [excess] of their toils, so that they 'die on you'—you mean, you kill them—mining gold for you day after day?"

Finally, Montesinos challenged all who heard him: "Are these Indians not men? Do they not have rational souls? Are you not obligated to love them as yourselves?" Montesinos accused the Spanish colonists of murder—the mass murder not of "savages," but of human beings. A storm of controversy followed.

With his simple questions Montesinos initiated the first significant clash between the Spaniards who came to the New World for gold and silver and those who came to serve the Indians. It was, of course, very much in the interests of the Conquistadors to hold that the Indian was a "savage" whose only real use was "digging for gold." Indeed, there were Christian missionaries who supported this position. Among them was Francisco Ruiz, who in 1517 stated:

> Indians are malicious people who are able to think up ways to harm Christians, but they are not capable of natural judg-

ment or of receiving the faith, nor do they have the other
virtues required for their conversion and salvation...and
they need, just as a horse or beast does, to be directed and
governed by Christians who treat them well and not cruelly.

In 1525 missionary Tomas Ortiz echoed Ruiz in stating: "God has
never created a race more full of vice....The Indians are more stupid
than asses and refuse to improve in anything." Perhaps the most negative description of the Indians, however, was that of the royal historian Gonzalo de Oviedo, who held that the Indians were "incapable
of becoming Christians" and testified that Indians were cannibals,
idolaters, and sodomites who readily committed suicide. (As noted in
the previous chapter, many Indians *did* commit suicide—as an act of
despair). Oviedo's early very negative "history" of the Indians laid
the foundation for the brutality of the Conquistadors.

There were also powerful voices that defended the humanity of
the Indians. One of the most important of these voices was that of
Bartolomé de Las Casas, who was mentioned earlier and will be dis-
cussed in the following section. Another important voice was that of
Pope Paul III (1468-1549) who in 1537 stated in *Sublimis Deus*
("The Sublime God") that

...the Indians and all other people who may later be discovered by Christians are by no means to be deprived of their
liberty or the possession of their property, even though they
be outside the faith of Jesus Christ; and...they may and
should, freely and legitimately, enjoy their liberty and the
possession of their property; nor should they be in any way
enslaved; should the contrary happen it shall be null and of
no effect.

Paul III declared clearly that "Indians are truly men" and followed this
with the admonition that any attempts at conversion were to be of a
nonviolent nature and were to be based on the good deeds of the
Spaniards. In his words: "...the said Indians and other peoples should
be converted to the faith of Christ by the preaching of God's word and
by the example of good and holy living."

Although Pope Paul III obviously did not support the use of military forces as agents to conquer or convert the Indians, this did not

settle the matter. The controversy inspired by Montesinos's rebuke of the colonizers in 1511 raged back and forth for several decades. A great deal was at stake in the outcome of the debate: if Indians were human beings who owned their own property, then they could not be enslaved; if they were "barbarians," then slavery was their natural condition. If Indians had souls, their gold was their own; if they were "savages," it belonged to the Spaniards.

It was here that former slave owner and later Dominican priest Bartolomé de Las Casas entered the debate. His intervention set the stage for an understanding of indigenous culture that was to serve as a powerful foundation for a Christian view of World Community.

Bartolomé de Las Casas

The anthropological and theological thought of Bartolomé de Las Casas (1484–1566) on the human rights of Indians and other slaves has had a profound influence on the Christian theology of World Community. Because, however, as a young man Las Casas personally owned Indian slaves, and in 1516 called for "some twenty black and other slaves" to be imported to the Americas, his standing as a human rights advocate has been disparaged by many and he has lost his proper place in history. As we shall see shortly, Las Casas sincerely repented for both of these "sins" and the major portion of his life was dedicated to ending *all* slavery: that of the Indians and later that of black Muslims and Africans as well. Las Casas preceded by several centuries the more popular anti-slave movements that dominated the nineteenth century.

For many years, much of Las Casas's work was virtually unknown. Only in the last century were many of his writings published and translated into English. Many people are still unaware of his contributions.

As noted above, Las Casas clearly had pivotal importance, not only for the eventual abolition of *all* slavery but also for the emerging Christian theology of World Community. It is essential to look at the whole trajectory of Las Casas's life, and to focus not on his ownership of Indian slaves or the importation of black slaves, but rather on what he did when he recognized the terrible error of his ways. Las Casas had the courage to admit his moral failings and to change.

For people who have the "courage to change," Bartolomé de Las Casas is a perfect model. Las Casas's experiences with the Indians and with his fellow Spaniards who enslaved them; his lifelong education in theology, philosophy, and law; and his persistence in seeking to live the gospel commend him to all who believe that humanity— with the conscience that guides it—is on a journey, not frozen in time and chained to the past.

The following is a brief outline of important years and events in Las Casas's life:

— 1484. Born in Seville, Spain. Bartolomé's father, Pedro, was a merchant who accompanied Columbus on his second voyage and became an estate owner and slave holder in the New World.

— 1502. Las Casas arrives on Hispaniola in the Caribbean to work at his father's *encomienda* (plantation). He witnesses the brutal suppression of the Indians and the harsh treatment of them in the mines and on the plantations.

— 1507. At age twenty-three, Las Casas is ordained a priest in Spain.

— 1512. Las Casas serves as chaplain for the Spanish invasion of Cuba.

— 1513. Las Casas is rewarded with his own plantation and slaves in Cuba.

— 1514. At age thirty, after being denied absolution in confession because he is a slave owner, Las Casas gives up his *encomienda* and dedicates the rest of his life to the liberation of the Indians.

— 1516. Las Casas calls for the importation of "some twenty black and other slaves" from Spain to replace Indians in the mines.

— 1522. Las Casas joins the Dominican order and is strongly influenced by the writing of Thomas Aquinas on natural law.

— 1527. Las Casas begins work on his *History of the Indies*, a work that explores the humanity of the Indians.

- 1542. Las Casas is influential in enacting the "new laws" that require the eventual end of the *encomienda* system of enslavement. Las Casas is called "the most hated man in the Indies."

- 1544. Las Casas becomes bishop of Chiapas (Mexico), where he refuses absolution to slave holders who do not promise restitution to the Indians. The colonists demand his dismissal.

- 1550–1551. The Las Casas/Sepulveda debate on whether the conquest of the Indians was a "just war" takes place in Valladolid, Spain.

- 1550s. Las Casas asks God to forgive him for his earlier acceptance of black slavery. He states that "blacks were enslaved unjustly, tyrannically, right from the start, exactly as the Indians had been." His condemnation includes the slavery of "Moors or Indians, or blacks or Arabs."

- 1556. Las Casas dies in Spain.

As is evident in this chronology, Bartolomé de Las Casas did not end his life as he began it. In his youth he witnessed the enslavement of human beings. Well into his thirties (even as a Catholic priest!) he either owned slaves or accepted their existence. This is why people in search of their own conscience on such grave issues as war and peace do well to reflect on Las Casas's pilgrimage to his own "inner light."

Las Casas and his supporters were not, in the end, victorious in their struggle to stop the vicious attacks on, and the enslavement of, the Indians in the New World. It would take centuries before some modicum of justice was achieved for the Indians in North and South America. But by the time that happened it was too late, as in the intervening period millions and millions had lost their lives, their property, their hope. Whole peoples were annihilated and great cultures were lost forever.

But Las Casas did leave behind a philosophical and anthropological heritage that inspired a theology of World Community and influenced the development of international law.

There are four principal ways in which Las Casas contributed to the philosophy of World Community: (1) The Law of Nations,

(2) Rejection of War, (3) Christ's Peaceful Way, and (4) Restorative Justice. Each contribution merits a brief discussion. (The quotes that follow are from *Bartolomé de Las Casas: The Only Way,* [1992].)

1. The Law of Nations. As we have seen, by characterizing the Indians as "barbarians" and "savages," the Conquistadors could hold that they were sub-human and, therefore, should not be treated as human beings. Las Casas argued in many places that the Indians *are* human beings, and are bound by the same natural law (which is rooted in the eternal law) that binds Europeans. Indeed, Las Casas realized that Indians are entitled to freedom and the ownership of their property that is recognized in what he called the "law of nations."

To make the point that Indians are subject to the law of nations, Las Casas described the quite sophisticated "political and social order" of the Indians:

> Then too there exist extraordinary kingdoms among our Indians who live in the regions west and south from us. There are large groupings of human beings who live according to a political and a social order. There are large cities, there are kings, judges, laws, all within civilizations where commerce occurs, buying and selling and lending and all the dealing proper to the law of nations. That is to say, their republics are properly set up, they are seriously run according to a fine body of law, there is religion, there are institutions. And our Indians cultivate friendship and they live in life-giving ways in large cities. They manage their affairs in them with goodness and equity, affairs of peace as well as war. They run their governments according to laws that are often superior to our own....

Las Casas went so far as to conclude that the Indians "... surpass the Greeks and Romans. They surpass the English, the French, and some groups in our native Spain." All of this was stated to make the point that the Indian nations enjoy the same rights as their European counterparts and that they should be treated justly and with respect. Las Casas noted emphatically that the Indians "have and hold their realms, their lands, by natural law and by the law of nations."

2. Rejection of War. War as a means to colonize Indians or to spread Christianity was absolutely rejected by Las Casas. He accepted the just war tradition but understood it as applying to wars against "tyranny." Consequently, he believed that the wars fought for "greed" and "gold" by the Conquistadors were in themselves tyrannical and, therefore, clearly immoral.

Las Casas discussed the counterproductive nature of war for "conversion" or "freedom" by pointing out how the Indians would react to those who would spread the "joyful tidings" of the gospel through war:

> What do joyful tidings have to do with wounds, captivities, massacres, conflagrations, the destruction of cities, and the common evils of war? They [the Indians] will go to hell rather than learn the advantages of the Gospel. And what will be told by the fugitives who seek out the provinces of other peoples out of fear of the Spaniards, with their heads split, their hands amputated, their intestines torn open? What will they think about the God of the Christians? They will certainly think that [the Spaniards] are sons of the devil, not the children of God and the messengers of peace.

Would the Indians, Las Casas asks, "want the truth to be announced to them after their homes have been destroyed, their children imprisoned, their wives raped, their cities devastated, their maidens deflowered, and their provinces laid waste?" He concludes by asking, "Where is humanity? Where is the meek and gentle spirit of Christ?"

3. Christ's Peaceful Way. For Las Casas there is another way to spread the gospel: the way of Christ. In his view, it is the way of "reason," "gentleness," "humility," "poverty," "compassion," "modesty," "respect"—a way "first by deeds, second by words." He tells us that "Christ is not violent. He is peaceable to all."

For Las Casas, the "peace" that is proclaimed by Christians is not the false peace that is produced by war or tyranny. He states that the disciples of Christ are "lovers of peace, messengers of peace" who spread the gospel "by the doctrine of Christ, which is fully gentle, fully peaceful, fully loving...." In *The Only Way* Las Casas explains

that "spiritual weapons" are the only effective means to spread the
Gospel:

> ...the weapons of war are physical things. Their nature is not
> to conquer souls but bodies, booty, buildings, material things
> they can reach. But it is through *spiritual weapons* that the
> Christian people are to be formed, gathered, settled, pre-
> served—the way Christ wanted and still wants to gather, set-
> tle, expand, preserve those over whom He wanted a spiritual
> rule, so they might become His by faith, hope, charity, virtues
> of the free soul only. By *spiritual arms*, i.e., by a Gospel mes-
> sage full of light, of gentleness, of kindness, by the sacra-
> ments, by the grace of the Holy Spirit, actual and habitual.

4. Restorative Justice. As a Dominican friar, Las Casas was well
schooled in the thought of Thomas Aquinas and, therefore, of Cicero, Aristotle, Augustine of Hippo, and many other commentators
on "pagan" and Christian ethics. In his reaction to the Conquistadors, therefore, Las Casas relied heavily on the ancient tradition that
a person has a moral obligation to restore stolen goods, and to repair
injuries done to others. Simply stated, one has a duty to "right" a
"wrong" done to another. This duty is variously called "restoration"
or "restitution."

Consequently, in *The Only Way* Las Casas comments on the duty
of restitution in the "wars of conversion" against the Indians:

> On the peril of losing their souls, all who start wars of con-
> version, all who will in the future, all who assist in any way
> that we just said, all are bound to restore to the devastated
> pagan peoples whatever they took in war, permanent or per-
> ishable, and make up for whatever they destroyed. Make up
> totally.

This is the "justice after war" *(ius post bellum)* principle that requires just compensation. Since Las Casas knew the "wretched wa-
gers of war" would not "make even the least satisfaction" for their
crimes against the Indians, he hoped at least for an admission of
guilt: "Would to God they could be sorry for their hideous crimes
before they die!"

The following are the contributions of Bartolomé de Las Casas to the World Community model:

- Natural law recognizes the human dignity of all cultures.
- Indians and other aboriginal people have inalienable rights.
- The law of nations governs relations between states.
- War as a method of conversion is immoral.
- Jesus' way of conversion is through gentleness and kindness.
- Restitution is mandatory for nations that fight unjust wars.

We turn now to a discussion of the contributions that Las Casas and his associates have made to an emerging world order.

The Legacy of Las Casas

Perhaps the most dramatic debate in the history of human rights took place in 1550 at Valladolid, Spain. The official topic of the disputation was whether the King of Spain could wage war on the Indians in the Americas in order to convert them to the Catholic faith. The participants were Bartolomé de Las Casas, who held that the Indians were "human beings," and Juan Gines de Sepulveda, who held that the Indians were the "natural slaves" of the Spaniards. Las Casas, of course, believed that the wars were criminal, since in his view the Indians had human rights that were rooted in natural law and the law of nations.

The debate was of historic significance, because nations at war are hardly prone to conduct a formal debate on the morality of the war *while it is still being fought.* In *All Mankind Is One* (1974), Lewis Hanke's study of the Valladolid debate, we read: "For the first time, and probably for the last, a colonizing nation organized a formal inquiry into the justice of the methods used to extend its empire." But the learned judges of the debate could not agree as to who had won the debate and, because of that, the question continued to be debated for the next several hundred years. Meanwhile, the Indians of South and North America suffered. They continued to be enslaved, tortured, and killed. Gold and silver and the fruits of slavery flowed into the hands of the Spanish crown and the Conquistadors, although very little ever reached the Spanish people. The Catholic

Church remained badly divided on the question, with some missionaries assisting in the conquest of the New World while others vigorously resisted it.

But not all was lost. Las Casas had a powerful influence on the development of what was to become contemporary international law. Since inalienable human rights are the foundation of all law, the effects of Las Casas's recognition of the natural rights of the Indians extend all the way to the United Nations Universal Declaration of Human Rights. In addition, Las Casas influenced the philosophers of international law and the academics and missionaries who were to labor in the New World. The following are some of the individuals who reflected Las Casas's concerns on international human rights:

Francisco de Vitoria (1486–1546). Perhaps the most direct influence that Las Casas had was on Francisco de Vitoria, a fellow Dominican friar who was a distinguished professor at the University of Salamanca. In a 1541 lecture entitled "On the Indies," Vitoria spoke out against the forced conversion of the Indians. He also refined the teaching on just war with very direct consequences for the unjust war against the Indians. Vitoria is credited having had a significant influence in the development of contemporary international law.

Francisco Borgia (1510–1572). Francisco Borgia was the third superior general of the newly founded Society of Jesus (Jesuits). Borgia, who studied at Salamanca, urged Pope Paul V to adopt policies that required the civil rulers in the New World to treat the Indians justly in order to convert them to Christianity. Later Jesuit missions *(Reducciones)* in South America were distinguished by their respect for the Indians and the creation of cooperative societies that were advocated by Las Casas. The missions failed in 1767 when Portuguese soldiers attacked the Indians and expelled the Jesuits.

Francisco Suarez (1548–1617). Francisco Suarez was a Spanish Jesuit who, like Las Casas, based his views on Aquinas's teaching on natural law. In "On War and the Indies," Suarez described the nations of the New World as independent states and rejected Spain's colonial system. In his publication "On Laws," Suarez wrote that a state's authority comes from the consent of the governed, thus refuting the "divine right of kings" theory. His view was that all people have a natural right to freedom and property. He is regarded as a "founder" of contemporary international law.

Hugo Grotius (1583–1645). Hugo Grotius was a Dutch Protestant jurist who is most famous for his *On the Law of War and Peace* (1625) that many regard as the blueprint for contemporary international law. Like Aquinas and Las Casas, Grotius's views on war and peace are rooted in natural law. Grotius accepts the notion of just war, but teaches, however, that the recognition of human rights on an international level will minimize the resort to war. He advocated freedom of the high seas and held that arbitration was an alternative to war. Grotius did not, however, attempt to abolish war, since it appears he accepted the reality that as long as there were nation states there would be war.

Immanuel Kant (1724–1804). Immanuel Kant was a German philosopher who held that people must be treated as "ends"—not "means"—and that ethical responsibility must be based on "duty." In *Perpetual Peace* (1795), Kant stated that the "civil constitution of every state should be republican [democratic]," and that "the law of nations shall be founded on a federation of free states." Kant's statement that "a violation of [human] rights in one place is felt throughout the world" prefigured Dr. Martin Luther King Jr.'s statement that "injustice anywhere is a threat to justice everywhere." Kant's prophetic vision strongly influenced the formation of the European Union in the twentieth century and continues to lay the philosophical foundation for World Community.

Through the centuries that followed, international law became a distinct field of study. Many of Las Casas's ideas can be found in humanistic and religious movements for liberation as well as in the philosophy of international law. Theologian Gustavo Gutiérrez, author of the classic *A Theology of Liberation* (1973), is one of several contemporary authors who have produced serious studies of Las Casas's view of international human rights and political freedom. Writing in *Las Casas: In Search of the Poor of Jesus Christ* (1992) Gutiérrez states:

The contribution of Las Casas is not limited to the debate—still quite heated until just a few years ago—regarding the colonization and the defense of the inhabitants of the continent that today we call America. His contribution has been decisive in the arenas of human rights, religious freedom, democratic institutions, and the effort to understand the "other" of Western civilization.

Las Casas also made significant contributions to what were to become the disciplines of anthropology and social psychology. His respect for the Indian character led him to deeply value their culture and high level of civilization. He was able to place himself inside the Indian mind and so understand, therefore, both the height of their spirituality and the depth of despair that drove some to suicide and violence.

The test of a great idea is not whether it succeeds in its own time but whether it has enduring value for all time. Las Casas's "great idea" that free human beings could live in a community characterized by harmony and justice failed in his own time. But the idea is not dead, since ideas as spiritual entities can never die.

The Seed Is Planted

Gradually, slowly, the idea of World Community emerged from Las Casas's struggle for Indian rights in the sixteenth century; from the beginnings of the philosophy of international law in seventeenth century; from the struggle to abolish slavery in the eighteenth century; from the nineteenth-century movement for women's suffrage; from the early twentieth-century efforts to form labor unions; and from the late twentieth-century environmental movement. Though each started with a specific focus, all of these great movements soon realized the global dimensions of their mission. Today almost all of these movements are international and are recognized by the United Nations as "non-governmental organizations" (NGOs).

The efforts of Bartolomé de Las Casas and of other missionaries and philosophers on behalf of the Indians served as an important foundation for the emerging field of international law. Soon advocates of international law were speaking not only of the rights of Indians but also of the rights of prisoners, victims, and noncombatants in war. Gradually the discussion extended to broader human rights issues and came to include even laws regulating commerce and the use of the oceans and other waterways. Eventually laws were created to regulate such practical matters as the delivery of international mail and the law of the sea. The seed had been planted.

The belief that people had "natural rights" resulted in political movements for independence (American, French, and South American revolutions) and the recognition that political minorities should be protected from the tyranny of the majority (similar to what is stated in the Bill of Rights in the American Constitution). The Catholic philosophy of natural law, the Puritan theology of direct inspiration, and the Quaker conviction that "there is of God in each of us" helped to spread the "radical" idea that individuals had worth, that they were important. Above all, both secular and religious thinkers agreed that each human person has a profound and sublime dignity that no law, no government, no authority could violate or deny.

While individuals contribute mightily to peace, the real work is done by organizations made up of countless anonymous men and women who are dedicated to this ideal and willing to work toward it, even by performing such simple tasks as addressing envelopes or printing flyers. The *Biographical Dictionary of Modern Peace Leaders* identifies over a hundred significant organizations founded since the nineteenth century that are dedicated to international peace and World Community. The following are examples: 1815: Massachusetts Peace Society; 1848: Universal Peace Congress; 1868: Universal Peace Society; 1892: International Peace Bureau; 1899: Hague Peace Conference; 1915: Fellowship of Reconciliation; 1919: Women's International League for Peace and Freedom; 1923: War Resisters International; 1945: Pax Christi International; 1947: United World Federalists; 1958: Campaign for Nuclear Disarmament; 1966: Stockholm International Peace Research Institute.

This is but a very small sample of the significant activity that has taken place throughout the world. Since the 1970s there have been scores of international meetings and conferences on disarmament, the environment, women's issues, globalization, human rights, and world federalism. Clearly, there is a vigorous citizen-based campaign to abolish war and to establish a governed world, or a least a world based on respect for international law.

Perhaps the most significant global conference on peace at the end of the twentieth century was the 1999 Hague Appeal for Peace. Over ten thousand people from hundreds of organizations around the world gathered in Holland to call for a new world order based on law and justice. The delegates sadly noted the death of more than one hundred million people—most of them civilians—killed in the wars of the twentieth century. National media outlets paid scant attention to this historic conference. Though events like this are little noticed, they are slowly, quietly laying the foundation for the type of global union that World Community advocates believe will be realized much sooner than many think—perhaps within the next hundred years!

Pacem in Terris—Peace on Earth

At the height of the Cold War (1945–1990), the United States and the Soviet Union came within minutes of a nuclear exchange that might have destroyed the world. In 1962, President John F. Kennedy (1917–1963) told Soviet leaders that if they did not remove their nuclear missiles from Cuba the United States was prepared to launch a "full retaliatory response" that included the use of nuclear weapons. Because both sides showed restraint and the Soviet leaders agreed to remove the weapons (on the condition that the U.S. also remove weapons close to the USSR), the world was saved from nuclear war.

Pope John XXIII (1881–1963) was deeply concerned by how close the world had come to extinction. Perhaps because of his own military experience in the Italian army in World War I, and because of his direct experience of World War II, the pope published the historic papal letter *Pacem in Terris*—"Peace on Earth" (1963). His concern was expressed in these words: "Therefore, in an age such as ours which prides itself on its atomic energy [weapons] it is contrary to reason to hold that war is now a suitable way to restore rights which have been violated." On the one hand, the pope was stating quite clearly that there can never be a "just" atomic war, while on the other he was offering a signal that he thought the Catholic Church should move beyond just war to adopt a new philosophy regarding war.

That new philosophy is Pope John's call for a "world-wide public authority" to solve global problems and to promote the "universal common good." The foundation of this papal letter, the first to be addressed to "all people of good will," is the philosophy of natural law. Pope John states: "But the Creator of the world has imprinted in man's heart an order which his conscience reveals to him and enjoins him to obey." The laws that govern people are from the "Father of all things" who wrote them in "the nature of man."

There are eight themes in *Pacem in Terris* that are central to the pope's call for a "world-wide public authority":

1. natural law confers on each human being inalienable rights that include freedom, association, a just wage, private property, and judicial protection;

2. people have corresponding duties that include the duty to seek truth, to live in community, and to cooperate for the common good;

3. public authority must safeguard human rights and enforce only laws that are based on the moral law;

4. states have an obligation to end the arms race, to abolish nuclear weapons, and to disarm;

5. the universal common good demands that international problems be solved by a global public authority;

6. the world-wide public authority must be freely chosen and not imposed by war;

7. the world-wide public authority must respect the proper authority of individual states;

8. the United Nations and the Universal Declaration of Human Rights (1948) are endorsed as "an important step on the path towards the juridical-political organization of all the peoples of the world."

The following quotations from *Pacem in Terris* expand on three of these themes.

The arms race must end:

> Justice, then, right reason and consideration for human dig-
> nity and life urgently demand that the arms race should
> cease; that the stockpiles which exist in various countries
> should be reduced equally and simultaneously by the par-
> ties concerned; that nuclear weapons should be banned; and
> finally that all come to an agreement on a fitting program
> of disarmament, employing mutual and effective controls.
> (112)

An international public authority is needed:

> Today the universal common good poses problems of world-
> wide dimensions, which cannot be adequately tackled or
> solved except by the efforts of public authority endowed
> with a wideness of powers, structure and means of the same
> proportions: that is, of public authority which is in a position
> to operate in an effective manner on a world-wide basis. The
> moral order itself, therefore, demands that such a form of
> public authority be established. (137)

The United Nations must be empowered to effectively protect "universal, inviolable and inalienable rights":

> It is therefore our ardent desire that the United Nations Or-
> ganization—in its structure and in its means—may become
> ever more equal to the magnitude and nobility of its tasks,
> and may the time come as quickly as possible when every
> human being will find therein an effective safeguard for the
> rights which derive directly from his dignity as a person, and
> which are therefore universal, inviolable and inalienable
> rights. This is all the more to be hoped for since all human
> beings, as they take an ever more active part in the public
> life of their own country, are showing an increasing interest
> in the affairs of all peoples, and are becoming more con-
> sciously aware that they are living members of the whole
> human family. (145)

In this letter, the pope is actually summarizing the long history of Catholic social thought and Christian humanism that has continually looked to structural reform as a solution to individual problems. That is, people often do evil things because the system they live under leaves them no alternative (unemployment invariably breeds crime, for example). When a new system is put in place (such as full employment), individual behavior changes for the better.

Hence, the main point of *Pacem in Terris* is that nations go to war in part because they lack international mechanisms to stop or prevent war. An international system that mandates diplomacy, mediation, arbitration, the use of a nonviolent army, a global police force, and the binding authority of the World Court and International Criminal Court can go a long way in preventing "rogue" nations from attacking others or in prosecuting world leaders who commit criminal acts. A new global judicial system with enforcement power can do much to prevent war.

Pope John XXIII also called the Second Vatican Council (1963–1965) in which the world's Roman Catholic bishops condemned war in the strongest terms and called for "the establishment of some universal public authority acknowledged as such by all, and endowed with effective power to safeguard, on the behalf of all, security, regard for justice, and respect for rights" (*Gaudium et Spes*, 82). Through the years Popes Paul VI and John Paul II have also vigorously condemned war and called for a new world order based on the principles of human rights and social justice. Both popes very specifically praised the United Nations and made personal visits to it. Pope Benedict XVI has indicated that he will continue this papal peace tradition.

The World Council of Churches

The World Council of Churches (WCC), from its inception in 1948, has given exceptional support to the United Nations and to the principles of World Community. The WCC is a fellowship of over 340 Protestant, Orthodox, and independent Christian churches found in more than one hundred countries and representing some four hundred million members. The WCC has long championed the creation of international institutions, international law, respect for human rights, the dignity of women, work for disarmament, and economic and social justice.

The WCC has been a leader in developing action programs for other NGO representatives to the United Nations. In the 1990s, the WCC strongly supported the World Conference on Environment and Development (Rio Earth Summit), the Copenhagen Social Summit, the Beijing World Conference on Women and Development, and the Cairo World Conference on Population and Development. The WCC was a prime mover in the creation of the International Criminal Court and serves on NGO committees that deal with social development, women, indigenous peoples, and children in armed conflict. Together, the Roman Catholic Church and the WCC strongly support the United Nations and the creation of a global public system that can defend justice and outlaw war.

A conscience that supports World Community can be securely rooted in the teachings of the Catholic Church and the World Council of Churches.

The World Federalist Movement

The World Federalist Movement (WFM) is an international organization that shares many of the ideals of the Christian churches on the quest for a governed world order. Since its foundation in 1947, the WFM has sought to end the international "anarchy" that reigns among nations and has sought to "invest legal and political authority in world institutions to deal with problems which can only be treated adequately at the global level, while affirming the sovereignty of the nation-state in matters which are essentially internal." The WFM seeks a "world governed by law, based on strengthened and democratized world institutions."

To this end, the WFM engages in five projects:

1. "Promoting Rule of Law, Defending Human Rights" (International Criminal Court, Universal Jurisdiction)

2. "Creating Lasting Peace, Preventing Conflicts—Protecting Civilians" (Humanitarian Intervention Debate, Combating Terrorism, Peace Education, Rapidly Deployable Peacekeeping Forces)

3. "Strengthening the United Nations" (Security Council Reform, UN Financing, Primacy of the General Assembly)

4. "More Democratic United Nations" (NGO Access, UN Reform, UN Parliamentary Assembly, Regional Democracy, Expanding Citizens Rights)

5. "Democratization of Globalization, Sustainable Development" (World Summit on Sustainable Development, Global Environmental Governance, World Environment Organization, WTO Parliamentary Assembly)

The World Federalist Movement is not alone in working for these goals. There are literally hundreds of UN NGOs that share the concerns of the WFM. Among them are the International Peace Bureau (1892) and the Hague Appeal for Peace (1999). Amnesty International (1961) has been particularly effective in its campaign for internationally recognized human rights. In addition, Quaker, Catholic, Jewish, Protestant, Humanist, Buddhist, Bahai, Hindu, Islamic, and other religious NGOs at the UN tirelessly promote the vision of a democratic world guided by spiritual values that promote international harmony.

International Organizations

The quest for World Community is not, however, a mere blueprint or abstract vision for the future. In fact, there already exist hundreds of international organizations that indicate that the future is partially here. The twentieth century witnessed spectacular growth in the number of international organizations dedicated to peace and justice between nations. While not all of these organizations were successful or have lived up to their lofty goals, their sheer existence is testimony to the desire of millions to move beyond the legal and moral straitjacket of the nation state.

After World War I (1914–1918) the League of Nations was formed to do what the Great War could not: end all war. Although the League had a World Court and a deliberative body, it lacked the essential enforcement powers that alone could prevent war. And so it collapsed before the marching boots of fascism in Italy, Japan, and Germany. The fact that the United States isolated itself from the world community and refused to join the League also contributed to its failure.

After World War II (1939–1945), the United Nations was founded "to unite our strength to maintain international peace and security." This time the United States *did* join the world community and the number of member states of the UN has risen from 51 in 1945, to 104 in 1961, to 191 in 2005. As a global body that represents just about every human person on the planet, the United Nations is a resounding success. Its dozens of unsung and under-studied agencies—from the familiar UNICEF (United Nations Children's Fund) to the obscure OHRLLS (Office of the High Representative for the Least Developed Countries, Landlocked Developing Countries and Small Island Developing States)—have achieved remarkable success in preventing dozens of wars and in promoting social justice around the world.

The United Nations, though it lacks essential legislative, judicial, and executive power, is the future already present among us. World Community advocates—including the great world's religions—look to the United Nations to become an effective political body that can abolish war through the enforcement of international law. Even a cursory glance at the organizational chart of the UN (available at www.un.org) tells us that the blueprint and the agencies for a "worldwide public authority" are already in place. World Community advocates believe that once these agencies are empowered by the member states through the vote of their citizens, peace can rapidly flourish throughout the world.

The future is already present in the many thousands of international organizations that have been created over the past hundred years. The *Yearbook of International Organizations* tells us that in 1909 there were a mere 213 NGOs and IGOs (inter-governmental organizations) in the world, while in 1999 there were 50,373 such bodies—an increase of 2,363 percent! In 1909 there were a handful of international meetings; according to *International Meeting Statistics for the Year 2003,* there were 7,978 international meetings in 2003 alone in Europe (58.3%), North America (14.9%), Asia (12.9%), South America (6.0%), Australasia/Pacific (3.1%), and Africa (4.8%). There were undoubtedly many more meetings, since this number is restricted to a minimum of 300 participants of whom 40 percent must be from outside the host country.

A great many of these organizations and meetings are concerned with policies and initiatives that promote World Community. In fact, there is a considerable body of international law that *already exists* on such matters as fair trade, communications, human rights, women's issues, weapons treaties, sea treaties, and outer space treaties. The United Nations, the activities of the NGOs and IGOs, and the thousands of international meetings each year tell us that the foundation for a World Community is already in place.

Finally, there is the remarkable story of the European Union. The European Union was first proposed in 1950 and was formally established in 1993. The idea of a united Europe dates back to the time of Julius Caesar (100–44 BCE), who conquered much of Europe with Rome's imperial armies. Charlemagne (ca. 742–814) ruled the Holy Roman Empire; Napoleon (1769–1821) and Adolf Hitler (1889–1945) for a short time ruled Europe through military conquest. The European Union has achieved through the rule of law what the great military commanders could not: peace through economic interdependence and shared government.

When Winston Churchill first proposed "a kind of United States of Europe" in 1946, people were either indifferent or amused. Some thought it a "silly idea" while others stated that it was "clearly impossible." But the fear of another war—this time with nuclear weapons—and the sheer economic devastation in every nation that resulted from World War II made a marriage of morality and necessity.

Spurred on by the American Marshall Plan in 1947, the European nations gradually began to rebuild their economies and, most important, to do so *interdependently*. Realizing that the destiny of one European nation was intimately entwined with the destiny of all, nations at first reluctant to cooperate eventually did so. The European Union was officially formed on November 1, 1993—less than fifty years after World War II. Today there are twenty-five nations, including many former Communist nations, in the European Union. Nations that had weapons pointed at each other just decades before now opened their borders to armies of tourists and workers. This, together with the nonviolent overthrow of so many Communist nations in 1989, is one of the true "miracles" of the twentieth century.

Why did this happen? Because it was an idea whose time had come. It was time to abandon hatred and war. It was time to abandon the mistaken philosophy that one nation is better than another. In the European Union, small nations like Ireland and Luxembourg are as secure and prosperous as large ones like Great Britain and Germany. The European currency, called the "euro," unites countries large and small on a continent that has learned, in the words of Albert Camus, to substitute "words" for "munitions."

Over the past fifty years those who have labored for the European Union have brought peace to Europe—a peace that some thought would not be achieved for five hundred years, if ever. When an idea meets its time, however, years become days and hours seconds. What great idea today walks among us searching for its time? Ideas are the most powerful forces in history when they have found the age that will accept them.

Terrorism and World Community

The terrorist events of September 11, 2001, that killed almost three thousand people caused advocates of World Community to redouble their efforts to work for a juridical world order. Although the method of attack was a surprise to World Community advocates, the attack on the United States was not. World Community analysts had known for some time (as had some governmental intelligence agencies) that the U.S. might be attacked because of frustration with U.S. policies toward Palestine and Islamic states in the Middle East. These analysts knew that the terrorists were the extremist "top" of a rather large mountain of Islamic resentment toward a thousand years of European militarism that had persecuted Muslims and exploited their natural resources. In the terrorists' view, the United States was merely continuing the European Crusades against Islam that were first promulgated in 1095.

Hence, World Community proponents did not find it useful to hear American political leaders claim that the terrorists had attacked because "they hate our freedom," or "they despise our way of life," or that we needed to mount a "Crusade" against Muslims. The terrorist attacks took place because the terrorists wanted to defend their own Islamic way of life, as well as to punish the Americans for their unjust policies in the Middle East. As unjust, as terrible, as counterproductive as the terrorist attacks were, they followed a reasoned policy to achieve political ends.

For World Community advocates, the attacks underscored the need for (1) a union of nations that would effectively prevent such attacks and (2) systemic changes in economic and social policy that would make such attacks unnecessary or impossible.

A World Community response to terrorism would endorse:

- *Preventive law.* While terrorism can best be prevented through just social policies, the role of intelligence services, the police, the courts, and the certainty of imprisonment must play a central role in preventing terrorist attacks. Arrest by local or global police forces, trial by the International Court of Criminal Justice or the World Court, and imprisonment will do much to deter terrorist individuals, groups, or nations from rogue or criminal actions. Terrorism will decline rapidly when terrorist leaders know for certain that they will be arrested and punished for their crimes.

- *A nonviolent army.* Force will often be necessary in the struggle against terrorism. Accordingly, a nonviolent peace force should be inserted into terrorist strongholds in order to compel the terrorists to cease their activities or to surrender. Just as nonviolent intervention was successful in so many instances in the twentieth century, it will be even more successful in the future, when we have a nonviolent army that has been professionally trained and is skilled in the strategies of nonviolence. Organizations such as Peace Brigades International can be quite useful in protecting civilians from terrorist attack. Some World Community advocates believe the use of violent force may also be necessary, but it must be used strictly as a last resort.

- *Social justice.* As with war, terrorism often results from the inability to settle differences through political discourse. Since the root causes of terrorism are often found among politically disenfranchised people, any attempt to engage in respectful dialogue (formally or informally) can be quite effective in reducing the perceived necessity for indiscriminate bloodshed. In addition to political powerlessness, other issues such as poverty and discrimination must also be addressed to efficiently deal with terrorism. Socially just societies tend to be nonviolent societies.

- *A peace culture.* All cultures revere those who give their lives for others. Some cultures restrict this respect to soldiers or military heroes who die in battle. Others—and their number is increasing—also honor nonviolent heroes who have demonstrated that there are many things they will die for, but nothing they will kill for. Schools can contribute to a global peace culture by studying both nonviolent "heroes" and the success of nonviolence in history. Athletes, artists, and intellectuals can reach across cultural divides to celebrate a common humanity. Religion can contribute to peace on earth by teaching that love and nonviolence can write the finest pages of human history.

Conclusion

The twentieth century was a remarkable century of death. It is conservatively estimated that forty-three million soldiers and sixty-two million civilians were killed in a century that began with the creation of the Nobel Peace Prize in 1901. And they may have been the lucky ones. Countless millions of survivors have had to live with shattered bodies and wrecked spirits. Millions of children have had to grow up without parents, and all the children of the world have grown up in the shadow of the mushroom cloud of atomic death that changed history forever in 1945. Further, although the United Nations was created in 1945 to "save succeeding generations from the scourge of war," just as many were to die after 1950 as before.

If these were the only statistics that survived that century, one could accurately conclude that war marked the human spirit and that peace was to be found only in romantic poetry. But there is hope. We do well to remember that the more than one hundred million people killed were in fact a fraction of the hundreds of millions of people who lived in peace in that century. Many nations did not fight at all, and people in countless families, villages, and cities lived in peace, even in nations at war. Throughout the century there were millions of acts of kindness, shared meals, rescues, and other expressions of human goodness and love that never made the newspapers or found their way into history books.

War or "military science" has long been a field of research, while the study of peace or "irenology" has littered the trash bin of what

Gene Sharp has called "disregarded history." Because we do not study peace, we think it is either nonexistent or impossible. But the field of peace research (with the allied fields of peace studies and peace education) emerged in the second half of the twentieth century with the comparative good news that war is neither natural to human beings nor is it inevitable. In fact, Gandhi was correct when he told us that "nonviolence is as old as the hills." For if war were the law of human nature, we would long ago have ceased to survive as a species. If at some point people had not stopped taking an "eye for an eye" or if they had not replaced "blood-letting" with "blood-sharing," the human race would have disappeared long ago. Peace may not be inevitable, but it is possible, and that alone can help us to attempt the seemingly impossible.

Advocates of World Community believe the remarkable success of the United Nations, the European Union, the international alliances that exist on every continent, and the many thousands of NGOs that are working for world peace provide ample motivation to take the next, final step: to end war itself. Some World Community advocates believe this can—and must—be accomplished in the next hundred years. Will the twenty-first century usher in a period of universal peace based on justice? It will if it heeds the words of Pope John XXIII in *Pacem in Terris*:

> There is reason to hope, however, that by meeting and negotiating, human beings may come to discover better the bonds that unite them together, deriving from the human nature which they have in common; and that they may also come to discover that one of the most profound requirements of their common nature is this: that between them and their respective peoples it is not fear which should reign but love, a love which tends to express itself in a collaboration that is loyal, manifold in form, and productive of many benefits. (129)

Two months after Pope John published those words in 1963, President John F. Kennedy lamented the "dangerous, defeatist belief" that peace was "impossible." In one of his last speeches as president, he offered words of hope to a generation that doubted it had a future. Kennedy's words recall a Christian humanism that is found in the writings of theologians and philosophers throughout Christian history:

Our problems are man-made. Therefore, they can be solved by man. And man can be as big as he wants. No problem of human destiny is beyond human beings. Man's reason and spirit have often solved the seemingly unsolvable—and we believe they can do it again.

Neither Pope John XXIII nor John F. Kennedy lived to see their vision of world peace fulfilled. Will world peace remain a dream denied?

The World Community Model: A Summary

The following are the key points that characterize a World Community model:

1. We are one human family. Every human being that is born is, without exception, a member of the species *homo sapiens*. All human beings have the same biological, psychological, and social needs and each person shares a common spiritual destiny with every other person. There is only one race: the human race. People should bear in mind, however, that as human beings they are a part of a larger web of life and so should live respectfully with other animals and with nature.

2. Cultural diversity should be celebrated. Although human beings share the same biological and psychological needs, it is natural for them to express themselves through different cultures that have distinctive languages, customs, artistic expressions, and religions. Diverse cultures that flow from a common humanity should be celebrated. Likewise, reverence for the diversity in the animal and plant world should be respected.

3. We need a global peace culture. Different cultures can unite in support of human rights, civil liberties, social justice, and nonviolence, which are the foundation of any civilized society. Peace can unite all cultures as they pursue security based on dialogue and cooperation. Annual *Pacem in Terris* awards can be given to the most peaceful village, city, province, or nation. The United Nations Universal Declaration of Human Rights can serve as the foundation for a global culture of peace.

4. We can create a world federal constitution. A world constitutional assembly can be called to enable the world's citizens to freely and democratically adopt a world federal constitution. National autonomy would be respected and an international body would be formed to resolve problems that cannot be handled at the national level. The constitution would establish freely elected legislative, judicial, and executive agencies sworn to resolve conflicts without recourse to war. A bill of rights would safeguard the rights of minorities and protect animals and the environment.

5. A global union can unite all. The world's citizens can elect representatives to a global union in accord with the world federal constitution. The global union would establish houses and ministers of government to justly represent the world's people, animals, and environment. Nation states would retain those rights not specifically delegated to the global union. A common currency that has the same value in every country could be established. Commerce would be based on the principles of social justice and environmental integrity.

6. A global police force can enforce international law. An international police force can be formed to enforce international law. The police would serve as "guardians of the peace" to intervene in those areas where national police prove to be ineffective or where they do not have proper jurisdiction. People would be presumed innocent until proven guilty and have a right to legal representation and a fair trial. Torture would be prohibited.

7. A nonviolent army can intervene to end violence. Since war would be forbidden by international law, a nonviolent army could be created to handle international disturbances or outbreaks of violence. This volunteer army would be trained in the philosophy and strategy of nonviolence and members would serve for a two-year period. The army would intervene directly between warring parties, employing the methods of resistance that would be most effective in settling particular disputes. In addition, citizens of every member nation would be trained in the methods of nonviolent civilian resistance against invasion or attack.

8. A global peace corps can promote social justice. A global peace corps would be established to maximize human rights and social justice in order to minimize violence and war. The activities of the global peace corps would include economic development, medical service, environmental stewardship, and education. Those in the global peace corps would receive the same salary and benefits as those in the nonviolent army.

9. Education can liberate all. Each citizen would be guaranteed free academic and professional education through the age of nineteen. Students pursuing undergraduate and postgraduate university education would receive free tuition along with a monetary stipend for living expenses. All students would have the opportunity to spend at least one year working or studying in another culture. Education would be considered a life-long experience; libraries would be expanded and courses of study would be provided for adults. Training in the theoretical and practical aspects of peacemaking would be available to all.

10. An annual world peace festival can be celebrated. A festival could be held each year to celebrate the foundation of the global union. The festival could feature troupes of athletes and artists who would travel the globe to remind all that sport and art have replaced violence and war. People of all lands and cultures would sing together, dance together, dine together, and meditate together to celebrate the fact that love is stronger than hate, and that hope is mightier than fear.

> *"We have it in our power to begin the world all over again."*
> Thomas Paine

———— • ————

This is your last letter to Nicole. The purpose of your letter is to help her better understand the concept of World Community by answering the following questions:

1. What is the biblical basis for World Community?

2. What is the teaching of Las Casas on World Community?

3. How did World Community develop in Christian history?

4. How does World Community respond to terrorism?

5. What, in your opinion, are the three most important key points in the World Community model?

You can now state your own view on World Community. What are its strong points? What are its weak points?

The information you provide on World Community in this final letter to Nicole will assist her to make an informed decision on her conscience and war. She will finally be able to arrive at a point where she can answer the question she posed at the beginning of this book: "Where do I stand on war?"

We turn, finally, to a discussion of where *you* stand on war.

Recommended Reading

The following books are recommended if you would like to learn more about World Community:

Elise Boulding. *Cultures of Peace: The Hidden Side of History*. Syracuse University Press, 2000.

Gustavo Gutiérrez. *Las Casas: In Search of the Poor of Jesus Christ*. Trans. Robert R. Barr. Orbis Books, 1993.

Gerald and Patricia Mische. *Toward a Human World Order: Beyond the National Security Straitjacket*. Paulist Press, 1977.

Joseph Rothblat, ed. *World Citizenship: Allegiance to Humanity*. St. Martin's Press, 1997.

Jonathan Schell. *The Unconquerable World: Power, Nonviolence, and the Will of the People*. Henry Holt and Company: Metropolitan Books, 2003.

Anne-Marie Slaughter. *A New World Order*. Princeton University Press, 2004.

PART THREE

War and Your Conscience

Where Do You Stand?

"Here I stand. I cannot do otherwise."
Martin Luther

Most people drift through life never knowing who they really are. When they look in the mirror they think they see a real person, but all they see is the image of a person that was created by their parents, or their religion, or their culture. If you ask them where they stand on something they will reply, "Oh, I stand here and there and if possible everywhere!" People want to please others, to be loved and accepted, to fit in.

Thus, the task of forming a conscience can be a very lonely journey that may lead to isolation and social ostracism. It can even lead to death. But the pilgrimage to conscience can also lead to happiness and serenity. It can lead to acceptance and love for oneself even though others may misunderstand or reject us.

In the end, people of conscience must be prepared to stand alone for what they hold sacred. However, in standing alone, they will gradually find that there are others who have stood with them throughout history, and who stand with them today. The call to conscience, while initially quite solitary, will in the end result in that which we all crave: community. "I rebel," said Albert Camus, "therefore *we* exist."

Who, really, are you? What, in your heart of hearts, are the convictions that you will live for? Die for? What great cause will you give your life to? You can go a long way in answering these questions by coming to an informed decision on where you stand with regard to war.

This book has attempted (1) to identify seven perspectives that form conscience and (2) to provide you with information on the four models or responses to war that have appeared in the course of Christian history. Once you determine how *you* should make moral decisions, you can then choose one model—or even a combination of several models—to express your position regarding war.

It is time, then, to write a letter to yourself.

There are two questions you need to answer: (1) How should I make moral decisions and (2) which of the four models best suits my conscience? The letters to Nicole that you wrote at the end of each chapter—on pacifism, just war, total war, and World Community—will greatly assist you in your task.

Here, in a bit more detail, is a process you may want to follow:

1. How should I make moral decisions?

In order to answer this question, you can once again prioritize the seven perspectives that form conscience to decide which are most important to you. Next to each of the following perspectives, which are listed in alphabetical order, place a number from 1 to 7, with 1 being the most important:

_____ CULTURE

_____ DUTY

_____ EGOISM

_____ GENDER

_____ RELIGION

_____ SCIENCE

_____ UTILITARIANISM

Be sure to number each perspective, since every one of them can assist you in forming a good conscience. Then write a brief paragraph about each perspective, explaining how it can help you decide what is ethical and what is not. The decisions you make about conscience will serve as the foundation for your view on war.

2. Where do I stand on war?

Now you can prioritize the four models that have been discussed in this book. Rank each of the following by using the numbers 1 through 4, with 1 representing your top choice:

_____ PACIFISM

_____ JUST WAR

_____ TOTAL WAR

_____ WORLD COMMUNITY

Some people may want to exclude one or more models as unethical, while others may want to combine several models. The best way to determine your own position is to review the ten key points that were listed at the end of each chapter. Hence, for example, a person could state, "I choose just war, but think that at times some aspects of the total war model may be acceptable" or "I believe in pacifism, but am willing to accept just war as a last resort if nonviolence fails."

Only you can determine where you stand. Keep a written record of your views on war. You may want to share it with your parents, teachers, religious leaders, or friends. You may even want to publish it. For those who might choose to seek conscientious objector status in the eventuality of a military draft or while on active duty, this written record will prove most helpful in documenting their claim before a draft board or review panel.

Those who decide for total war could find to their surprise that, because they reject just war principles or the restrictions on warfare that are imposed by the Geneva Convention, they may actually have difficulty in the armed forces. (There is, however, no way for a government to know this before one enlists in the military, since few questions are asked of those who join voluntarily.) The fact is that there are very strict moral and legal laws that apply to military service, which is why soldiers, even in combat zones, can be accused of murder.

Finally, if you would like to publish either the letters to Nicole that you wrote at the end of each chapter and/or the letter to yourself, you can consider a newspaper, or a magazine, or an Internet site that might be interested in publishing your work. This way you can receive feedback from others and continue to fine-tune your position on war.

Thank you for reading this book! I hope you have learned something and that you have found the information helpful in forming your conscience on war. If you are still confused, be patient with yourself. Read more, think more, meditate more, pray more. Talk with others, share your concerns, play with ideas. Your future, and that of many others, very much depends on where you stand on war.

And, finally, what about Nicole? What should she do?

Now I can tell you, dear reader, Nicole is *you*. As you decide, she decides. The heart of this wonderful young woman beats in of each of us. Be kind to Nicole; be kind to yourself; be kind to all.

Sources Consulted

A wide variety of sources was used in writing this book. In addition to the books listed below, these sources include scholarly journals, encyclopedias, and, of course the Internet. The inclusion of all these sources would overburden a book that is directed to the popular reader. Accordingly, the sources below are limited to books.

The entire text benefited from insights contained in Roland Bainton's *Christian Attitudes toward War and Peace: A Historical Survey and Critical Re-evaluation* (Abingdon, 1960), Lisa Sowle Cahill's *Love Your Enemies: Discipleship, Pacifism, and Just War Theory* (Fortress Press, 1994), Eileen Egan's *Peace Be with You: Justified Warfare or the Way of Nonviolence* (Orbis Books, 1999), and Ronald G. Musto's *The Catholic Peace Tradition* (Orbis Books, 1986; reprint ed. Peace Books, 2002) and his two-volume *Catholic Peacemakers: A Documentary History* (Garland, 1993, 1996). But it should be stressed that all of the books that are listed under each model helped put that tradition in proper perspective.

Please note that, in the listings that follow, citations for certain works do not include a publisher. These books are widely available and can generally be found in any bookstore, or in anthologies, or on the Internet.

Conscience

Thomas Aquinas. *Summa Theologica.*
Aristotle. *Nicomachean Ethics.*
Ruth Benedict. *Patterns of Culture.* Pelican, 1946.
Claudia Card, ed. *Feminist Ethics.* University of Kansas Press, 1991.
James Fieser. *Metaethics, Normative Ethics, and Applied Ethics: Historical and Contemporary Readings.* Wadsworth, 2000.
Stanley Hauerwas. *The Peaceable Kingdom: A Primer in Christian Ethics.* University of Notre Dame Press, 1983.
Pat Duffy Hutcheon. *The Road to Reason: Landmarks in the Evolution of Humanist Thought.* Canadian Humanist Publications, 2001.

Immanuel Kant. *Critique of Pure Reason.*

Alasdair MacIntyre. *After Virtue.* Notre Dame University Press, 1981.

Barbara MacKinnon. *Ethics: Theory and Contemporary Issues.* Wadsworth, 2004.

John Macquarrie, ed. *Dictionary of Christian Ethics.* The Westminster Press, 1967.

Daniel C. Maguire. *The Moral Code of Judaism and Christianity.* Fortress Press, 1993.

John Stuart Mill. *Utilitarianism.*

Plato. *The Republic.*

Louis P. Pojman. *How Should We Live? An Introduction to Ethics.* Wadsworth, 2005.

Scott B. Rae. *Moral Choices: An Introduction to Ethics.* Zondervan Publishing House, 2000.

Ayn Rand. *The Virtue of Selfishness.* New American Library, 1964.

Ninian Smart. *World Philosophies.* Routledge, 2000.

John Somerville and Ronald E. Santoni, eds. *Social and Political Philosophy.* Anchor/Doubleday, 1963.

James P. Sterba. *Ethics: Classical Western Texts in Feminist and Multicultural Perspectives.* Oxford University Press, 2000.

Model 1: Pacifism

David Anderson and Andrew Bolton. *Military Service, Pacifism, and Discipleship: A Diversity of Callings.* Community of Christ, 2003.

Thomas Aquinas. *Summa Theologica.*

Roland Bainton. *Christian Attitudes toward War and Peace: A Historical Survey and Critical Re-evaluation.* Abingdon, 1960.

Gregg Barak. *Violence and Nonviolence: Pathways to Understanding.* Sage Publications, 2003.

Peter Brock. *Varieties of Pacifism: A Survey from Antiquity to the Outset of the Twentieth Century.* Syracuse University Press, 1998.

Dale W. Brown. *Biblical Pacifism.* 2nd ed. Herald Press and Evangel Publishing House, 2003.

C. John Cadoux. *The Early Christian Attitude toward War.* The Seabury Press, 1982

Lisa Sowle Cahill. *Love Your Enemies: Discipleship, Pacifism, and Just War Theory.* Fortress Press, 1994

Conscientious Objectors and the Draft. The Center on Conscience and War, 2002.

John Dominic Crossan. *Jesus: A Revolutionary Biography.* Harper Collins, 1994.

Lawrence Cunningham. *Brother Francis*. Family Library, 1972.

John Dear. *Disarming the Heart*. Paulist Press, 1987.

John P. Dolan. *The Essential Erasmus*. The New American Library, 1964.

William Eckhardt. *Civilizations, Empires and Wars: A Quantitative History of War*. McFarland and Company, Inc., 1992.

Eileen Egan. *Peace Be with You: Justified Warfare or the Way of Nonviolence*. Orbis Books, 1999.

Robert Ellsberg. *All Saints: Daily Reflections on Saints, Prophets, and Witnesses for Our Time*. Crossroad Publishing Company, 1997.

John Ferguson. *The Politics of Love: The New Testament and Non-Violent Revolution*. James Clarke Publishers, 1970.

Andrew Fiala. *Practical Pacifism*. Algora Publishing, 2004.

W. H. C. Frend. *The Rise of Christianity*. Fortress Press, 1984.

Joseph Grassi. *Broken Bread and Broken Bodies: The Lord's Supper and World Hunger*, rev. ed. Orbis Books, 2004.

Chris Hedges. *War Is a Force That Gives Us Meaning*. Public Affairs, 2002.

Jean-Michel Hornus. *It Is Not Lawful for Me to Fight*. Herald Press, 1980.

Jewish Peace Fellowship. *Wrestling with Your Conscience: A Guide for Jewish Draft Registrants and Conscientious Objectors*. Fellowship of Reconciliation, 2000.

Pope John XXIII. *Pacem in Terris*. 1963.

Harold Josephson. *Biographical Dictionary of Modern Peace Leaders*. Greenwood Press, 1985.

John Keegan. *A History of Warfare*. Alfred A. Knopf, 1994.

Raymond C. Kelly. *Warless Societies and the Origin of War*. University of Michigan Press, 2003.

G. H. C. MacGregor. *The New Testament Basis of Pacifism*. Fellowship of Reconciliation, 1936.

Peter Mayer, ed. *The Pacifist Conscience*. Henry Regnery Company, 1971.

Neil B. McLynn. *Ambrose of Milan: Church and Court in a Christian Capital*. University of California Press, 1994.

Richard B. Miller. *Interpretations of Conflict: Ethics, Pacifism, and the Just-War Tradition*. University of Chicago Press, 1993.

Charles C. Moskos and John Whiteclay Chambers II, eds. *The New Conscientious Objection: From Sacred to Secular Resistance*. Oxford University Press, 1993.

John A. Mourant and William J. Collinge, trans. *Saint Augustine: Four Anti-Pelagian Writings*. The Catholic University of America Press, 1992.

Ronald G. Musto. *The Catholic Peace Tradition*. Orbis Books, 1986; reprint ed. Peace Books, 2002.

Ronald G. Musto. *Catholic Peacemakers: A Documentary History*. 2 vols. Garland Publishing, Inc., 1993, 1996.

Edgar W. Orr. *Christian Pacifism*. The C. W. Daniel Company Ltd., 1958.

Peter C. Phan. *Social Thought*. Michael Glazier, Inc., 1984.

Rosalie G. Riegle. *Dorothy Day: Portraits by Those Who Knew Her*. Orbis Books, 2003.

Lillian Schlissel, ed. *Conscience in America: A Documentary History of Conscientious Objection in America 1757–1967*. E. P. Dutton & Co., Inc., 1968.

Robert A. Seeley. *Choosing Peace: A Handbook on War, Peace, and Your Conscience*. Central Committee for Conscientious Objectors, 1994.

Mulford Q. Sibley, ed. *The Quiet Battle: Writings on the Theory and Practice of Non-Violent Resistance*. Beacon Press, 1963.

David R. Smock. *Religious Perspectives on War*. Rev. ed. United States Institute of Peace, 2002.

Louis J. Swift. *The Early Fathers on War and Military Service*. Michael Glazier, Inc., 1983.

Leo Tolstoy. *The Kingdom of God Is Within You*. University of Nebraska Press, 1984.

Andre Trocme. *Jesus and the Nonviolent Revolution*. Orbis Books, 2003.

Adolf von Harnack. *Militia Christi: The Christian Religion and the Military in the First Three Centuries*. Fortress Press, 1981. (Translated from the German edition originally published in 1905.)

Stephen Williams and Gerard Friell. *Theodosius: The Empire at Bay*. Yale University Press, 1994.

Walter Wink. *Engaging the Powers: Discernment and Resistance in a World of Domination*. Fortress Press, 1992.

Walter Wink. *Jesus and Nonviolence: A Third Way*. Fortress Press, 2003.

Wrestling with Your Conscience: A Guide for Jewish Draft Registrants and Conscientious Objectors. Jewish Peace Fellowship, 2000.

John Howard Yoder. *The Politics of Jesus*. 2nd ed. Eerdmans, 1994.

Howard Zinn, ed. *The Power of Nonviolence: Writings by Advocates of Peace*. Beacon Press, 2002.

Rachel S. Zuses, ed. *Words of Conscience: Religious Statements on Conscientious Objection*. 11th ed. The Center on Conscience and War, 2001.

Model 2: Just War

Thomas Aquinas. *Summa Theologica*.

Augustine of Hippo. *The City of God*.

Roland H. Bainton. *Christian Attitudes toward War and Peace: A Historical Survey and Critical Re-evaluation*. Abingdon, 1960.

Benedict Bauer. *Frequent Confession*. St. Paul Publications, 1959.

Joanna Bourke. *An Intimate History of Killing: Face to Face Killing in 20th Century Warfare*. Basic Books, 1999.

Peter Brown. *Augustine of Hippo*. University of California Press, 1969.

Lisa Sowle Cahill. *Love Your Enemies: Discipleship, Pacifism, and Just War Theory*. Fortress Press, 1994.

Darrell Cole. *When God Says War Is Right: The Christian Perspective on When and How to Fight*. Waterbrook Press, 2003.

John P. Dolan. *The Essential Erasmus*. The New American Library, 1964.

William Eckhardt. *Civilizations, Empires and Wars: A Quantitative History of War*. McFarland & Company, Inc., 1992.

Eileen Egan. *Peace Be with You: Justified Warfare or the Way of Nonviolence*. Orbis Books, 1999.

Daniel Ellsberg. *Secrets: A Memoir of Vietnam and the Pentagon Papers*. Viking, 2002.

Jean Bethke Elshtain. *Just War against Terror: The Burden of American Power in a Violent World*. Basic Books, 2003.

George W. Forell, ed. *Christian Social Teachings: A Reader in Christian Social Ethics from the Bible to the Present*. Doubleday, Anchor, 1966.

Shannon E. French. *Code of the Warrior: Exploring Warrior Values Past and Present*. Rowman & Littlefield Publishers, 2003.

James J. Greene and John P. Dolan, eds. *The Essential Thomas More*. The New American Library, A Mentor-Omega Book, 1967.

Dave Grossman. *On Killing: The Psychological Cost of Learning to Kill in War and Society*. Little, Brown and Company, Back Bay Books, 1996, 1995.

Dan Hallock. *Bloody Hell: The Price Soldiers Pay*. The Plough Publishing House, 1999.

Anthony E. Hartle. *Moral Issues in Military Decision Making*. Rev. ed. University Press of Kansas, 2004.

Chris Hedges. *War Is a Force That Gives Us Meaning*. Public Affairs, 2002.

James Turner Johnson. *Morality and Contemporary Warfare*. Yale University Press, 1999.

Richard W. Kaeuper. *Chivalry and Violence in Medieval Europe*. Oxford University Press, 2001.

John Keegan. *A History of Warfare*. Alfred A. Knopf, 1994.

C. H. Lawrence. *Medieval Monasticism*. Longman, 1984.

John Mahoney. *The Making of Moral Theology: A Study of the Roman Catholic Tradition*. Oxford University Press, 1987.

Neil B. McLynn. *Ambrose of Milan: Church and Court in a Christian Capital*. University of California Press, 1994.

Robert Meager. *Augustine: An Introduction*. New York University Press, 1978.

Thomas Merton (ed. Patricia A. Burton). *Peace in the Post-Christian Era*. Orbis Books, 2004.

E. B. F. Midgley. *The Natural Law Tradition and the Theory of International Relations*. Harper and Row Publishers, Inc., Barnes and Noble Import Division, 1975.

Richard B. Miller, ed. *War in the Twentieth Century*. Westminster/John Knox Press, 1992.

Ronald G. Musto. *The Catholic Peace Tradition*. Orbis Books, 1986; reprint ed. Peace Books, 2002.

Ronald G. Musto. *Catholic Peacemakers: A Documentary History*. 2 vols. Garland Publishing, Inc., 1993, 1996.

Terry Nardin, ed. *The Ethics of War and Peace: Religious and Secular Perspectives*. Princeton University Press, 1996.

Susan Niditch. *War in the Hebrew Bible: A Study in the Ethics of Violence*. Oxford University Press, 1993.

Reinhold Niebuhr. *Moral Man and Immoral Society*. Charles Scribner's Sons, 1932.

David J. O'Brien and Thomas A. Shannon, eds. *Catholic Social Thought: The Documentary Heritage*. Orbis Books, 1992.

Brian Orend. *War and International Justice: A Kantian Perspective*. Wilfrid Laurier University Press, 2000.

Pontifical Council for Justice and Peace. *Compendium of the Social Doctrine of the Church*. Libreria Editrice Vaticana, 2004. (Published by the United States Conference of Catholic Bishops, 2005.)

Paul Ramsey. *The Just War: Force and Political Responsibility*. Rowman & Littlefield, 1968, 1983.

W. Michael Reisman and Christ T. Antoniou. *The Laws of War: A Comprehensive Collection of Primary Documents on International Laws Governing Armed Conflict*. Vintage Books, 1994.

Frederick H. Russell. *The Just War in the Middle Ages*. Cambridge University Press, 1975.

David R. Smock. *Religious Perspectives on War*. Rev. ed. United States Institute of Peace, 2002.

J. Stevenson. *Creeds, Councils and Controversies: Documents Illustrative of the History of the Church A.D. 337–461*. S.P.C.K., 1966.

Peter S. Temes. *The Just War: An American Reflection on the Morality of War in Our Time*. Ivan R. Dee, 2003.

Joan D. Tooke. *The Just War in Grotius and Aquinas*. S.P.C.K., 1965.

Training Support Package 158-C-1131. *Apply Just War Tradition to Your Service as a Leader and the Profession of Arms*. U.S. Army Command and General Staff College, 1998.

Training Support Package 181-L-1001. *Conduct Small Unit Combat Operations According to the Law of War*. The Judge Advocate General's School, 1999.

The United States Marine Corps. *Warfighting: The U.S. Marine Corps Book of Strategy*. Currency Doubleday, 1994.

John A. Vasquez, ed. *What Do We Know About War?* Rowman & Littlefield Publishers, Inc., 2000.

Carl von Clausewitz. *On War*. Penguin Books, 1982.

Michael Waltzer. *Just and Unjust Wars: A Moral Argument with Historical Illustrations*. Basic Books, 1977.

George Weigel. *Tranquilitas Ordinis: The Present Failure and Future Promise of American Catholic Thought on War and Peace*. Oxford University Press, 1987.

William Allen White, ed. *Defense for America*. The Macmillan Company, 1940.

Garry Wills. *Saint Augustine's Sin*. Viking, 2003.

John Howard Yoder. *When War Is Unjust: Being Honest in Just-War Thinking*. Rev. ed. Orbis Books, 1984.

Daniel S. Zupan. *War, Morality and Autonomy: An Investigation in Just War Theory*. Ashgate Publishing, 2004.

Model 3: Total War

Fred Anderson and Andrew Cayton. *The Dominion of War: Empire and Liberty in North America 1500–2000*. Viking, 2005.

Alfred J. Andrea. *Encyclopedia of the Crusades*. Greenwood Press, 2003.

Christon I. Archer, John R. Ferris, Holger H. Herwig, and Timothy H. E. Travers. *World History of Warfare*. University of Nebraska Press, 2002.

Hannah Arendt. *The Origins of Totalitarianism*. Harcourt, Inc., A Harvest Book, 1994.

Karen Armstrong. *Holy War: The Crusades and Their Impact on Today's World*. Anchor Books, 2001.

Meg Bogin. *The Women Troubadours*. W. W. Norton, 1976.

E. R. Chamberlin. *The Bad Popes*. Dorset Press, 1969.

Noam Chomsky and Edward S. Herman. *The Washington Connection and Third World Fascism*. South End Press, 1979.

Henri Daniel-Rops. *Cathedral and Crusade*. Image Books, 1963.

Eileen Egan. *Peace Be with You: Justified Warfare or the Way of Nonviolence*. Orbis Books, 1999.

Barbara Ehrenreich. *Blood Rites: Origins and History of the Passions of War*. Henry Holt and Company, 1996.

Bill Fawcett, ed. *Mercs: True Stories of Mercenaries in Action*. Avon Books, 1999.

Shannon E. French. *The Code of the Warrior: Exploring Warrior Values Past and Present*. Rowman & Littlefield Publishers, Inc., 2003.

Daniel Hallock. *Hell, Healing and Resistance: Veterans Speak*. Plough, 1998.

B. H. Liddell Hart. *Strategy*. Praeger, 1954.

Richard Shelly Hartigan. *The Forgotten Victim: A History of the Civilian*. Precedent Publishing, Inc., 1982.

Adolf Hitler. *Mein Kampf*. Houghton Mifflin Company, 1971.

Hammond Innes. *The Conquistadors*. Knopf, 1969.

James Turner Johnson. *The Holy War Idea in Western and Islamic Traditions*. Pennsylvania State University Press, 2001.

David E. Jones. *Women Warriors: A History*. Brassey's, 1997.

Richard W. Kaeuper. *Chivalry and Violence in Medieval Europe*. Oxford University Press, 1999.

Herman Kahn. *On Thermonuclear War*. Greenwood Publishing Group, 1978. (Originally published in 1960.)

John Keegan. *A History of Warfare*. Alfred A. Knopf, 1993.

Tim LaHaye and Thomas Ice. *Charting the End Times: A Visual Guide to Bible Prophecy and Its Fulfillment*. Harvest House Publishers, 2001.

Tim LaHaye and Jerry B. Jenkins. *Armageddon*. Tyndale House Publishers, 2006. (This is part of the Left Behind series.)

Bartolomé de las Casas. *In Defense of the Indians*. Northern Illinois University Press, 1974.

George M. Mardsen. *Fundamentalism and American Culture: The Shaping of Twentieth-Century Evangelicalism 1870–1925*. Oxford University Press, 1980.

Tomaz Mastnak. *Crusading Peace: Christendom, the Muslim World, and Western Political Order*. University of California Press, 2002.

Maria Rosa Menocal. *The Ornament of the World: How Muslims, Jews, and Christians Created a Culture of Tolerance in Medieval Spain*. Little, Brown and Company, 2002.

Ronald G. Musto. *The Catholic Peace Tradition*. Orbis Books, 1986; reprint ed. Peace Books, 2002.

Ronald G. Musto. *Catholic Peacemakers: A Documentary History*. 2 vols. Garland, 1993, 1996.

Terry Nardin, ed. *The Ethics of War and Peace: Religious and Secular Perspectives*. Princeton University Press, 1996.

The Oxford Illustrated History of the Crusades. Ed. Jonathan Riley-Smith. Oxford University Press, 1995.

Gabriel Palmer-Fernandez and Ian Maclean, eds. *Encyclopedia of Religion and War*. Routledge Taylor and Francis Group, 2003.

Robert O. Paxton. *The Anatomy of Fascism*. Alfred A. Knopf, 2004.

Mary Elizabeth Perry and A. Cruz, eds. *Cultural Encounters: The Impact of the Inquisition in Spain and the New World*. University of California Press, 1991.

Karl R. Popper. *The Open Society and Its Enemies*, vol. 1: The Spell of Plato. Princeton University Press, 1962.

Samantha Power. *"A Problem from Hell": America and the Age of Genocide*. Perennial, Harper Collins Publishers, 2002.

Kirkpatrick Sale. *The Conquest of Paradise: Christopher Columbus and the Columbian Legacy*. Knopf, 1990.

Kenneth M. Setton, gen. ed. *A History of the Crusades.* 4 vols. University of Wisconsin Press, 1965.

P. W. Singer. *Corporate Warriors: The Rise of the Privatized Military Industry.* Cornell University Press, 2003.

Samuel A. Southworth. *U.S. Special Forces: A Guide to America's Special Operations Units—The World's Most Elite Fighting Force.* De Capo Press, 2002.

Tom Stonier. *Nuclear Disaster.* Penguin Books, 1964.

Palmer A. Throop. *Criticism of the Crusade: A Study of Public Opinion and Crusade Propaganda.* Porcupine Press, 1975. (Originally published in Amsterdam by N. V. Swets & Zeitlinger, 1940.)

Christopher Tyerman. *The Invention of the Crusades.* University of Toronto Press, 1998.

Alfred Vagts. *A History of Militarism: Civilian and Military.* Rev. ed. The Free Press, 1959.

Ludwig von Mises. *Omnipotent Government: The Rise of the Total State and Total War.* Libertarian Press, 1985.

Daniel Wojcik. *The End of the World as We Know It: Faith, Fatalism, and Apocalypse in America.* New York University Press, 1997.

Quincy Wright. *A Study of War.* University of Chicago Press, 1965.

John Howard Yoder. *When War Is Unjust: Being Honest in Just-War Thinking.* Rev. ed. Orbis Books, 1996.

Model 4: World Community

Esref Aksu and Joseph A. Camilleri. *Democratizing Global Governance.* Palgrave Macmillan, 2002.

Bartolomé de Las Casas: The Only Way. Ed. Helen Rand Parish, trans. Francis Patrick Sullivan, S.J. Paulist Press, 1992.

Elizabeth Bomberg and Alexander Subb. *The European Union: How Does It Work?* Oxford University Press, 2003.

Elise Boulding. *Building a Global Civil Culture: Education for an Independent World.* Syracuse University Press, 1988.

Elise Boulding. *Cultures of Peace: The Hidden Side of History.* Syracuse University Press, 2000.

Joseph A. Camilleri, Kamal Malhotra, Majid Tehranian, Project Directors. *Reimagining the Future: Towards Democratic Governance.* The Department of Politics, La Trobe University, 2000.

Catholic Association for International Peace. *The Role of the Christian in the World for Peace.* Washington, DC, 1953.

Center for the Study of Democratic Institutions. *A Constitution for the World.* 1965.

Nigel Dower. *An Introduction to Global Citizenship*. Edinburgh University Press, 2003.

Julie Fisher. *Nongovernments: NGOs and the Political Development of the Third World*. Kumarian Press, 1998.

Joseph Grassi. *Peace on Earth: Roots and Practices from Luke's Gospel*. Liturgical Press, 2004.

Gustavo Gutiérrez. *Las Casas: In Search of the Poor of Jesus Christ*. Trans. Robert R. Barr. Orbis Books, 1993.

Lewis Hanke. *All Mankind Is One*. Northern Illinois University Press, 1974.

Chris Hedges. *War Is a Force That Gives Us Meaning*. Public Affairs, 2001.

Pope John XXIII. *Pacem in Terris*. 1963.

Harold Josephson, ed. *Biographical Dictionary of Modern Peace Leaders*. Greenwood Press, 1985.

Immanuel Kant. *Perpetual Peace*. Macmillan Publishing Company, 1957.

Charles W. Kegley, Jr., and Gregory A. Raymond. *How Nations Make Peace*. St. Martin's Press, 1999.

Martin Luther King, Jr. *Why We Can't Wait*. A Mentor Book, New American Classics, 1963.

Chung Ok Lee, ed. *Vision for a New Civilization: Spiritual and Ethical Values in the New Millennium*. Won Buddhist Publishing, 2000.

Ralph B. Levering and Miriam L. Levering. *Citizen Action for Global Change: The Neptune Group and the Law of the Sea*. Syracuse University Press, 1999.

H. R. Loyn, ed. *The Middle Ages: A Concise Encyclopedia*. Thames and Hudson, Ltd., 1989.

Thomas J. Massaro and Thomas A. Shannon, eds. *American Catholic Social Teaching*. A Michael Glazier Book, Liturgical Press, 2002.

E. B. F. Midgley. *The Natural Law Tradition and the Theory of International Relations*. Harper and Row Publishers, Inc., Barnes and Noble Import Division, 1975.

Gerald and Patricia Mische. *Toward a Human World Order: Beyond the National Security Straitjacket*. Paulist Press, 1977.

Patricia M. Mische and Melissa Merkling, eds. *Toward A Global Civilization? The Contribution of Religions*. Peter Lang Publishing, Inc., 2001.

Hans J. Morgenthau, revised by Kenneth W. Thompson. *Politics Among Nations: The Struggle for Power and Peace*. 6th ed. McGraw-Hill, Inc., 1985.

Yeshua Moser-Puangsuwan. *Nonviolent Intervention Across Borders: A Recurrent Vision*. University of Hawaii Press, 2000.

Ronald G. Musto. *The Catholic Peace Tradition*. Orbis Books, 1986; reprint ed. Peace Books, 2002.

Ronald G. Musto, ed. *Catholic Peacemakers: A Documentary History: From the Renaissance to the Twentieth Century*, vol. 2, parts 1 and 2. Garland Publishing, 1993, 1996.

National Conference of Catholic Bishops. *The Challenge of Peace: God's Promise and Our Response.* United States Catholic Conference, 1983.

David J. O'Brien and Thomas A. Shannon. *Catholic Social Thought: The Documentary Heritage.* Orbis Books, 1992.

Brian Orend. *War and International Justice: A Kantian Perspective.* Wilfred Laurier University Press, 2000.

Anthony Pagden and Jeremy Lawrance. *Vitoria: Political Writings.* Cambridge University Press, 1991.

John Pinder. *The European Union: A Very Short Introduction.* Oxford University Press, 2001.

Pontifical Council for Justice and Peace. *Compendium of the Social Doctrine of the Church.* Libreria Editrice Vaticana, 2004. (Published by the United States Conference of Catholic Bishops, 2005.)

Roger S. Powers and William B. Vogele, eds; Christopher K. Kruegler and Ronald M. McCarthy, associate eds. *Protest, Power, and Change: An Encyclopedia of Nonviolent Action from ACT-UP to Women's Suffrage.* Garland Publishing, 1997.

Emery Reves. *The Anatomy of Peace.* Dallas Symphony Association, Inc., 1994. (Originally published in 1945.)

Adam Roberts and Richard Guelff, eds. *Documents on the Laws of War.* 3rd ed. Oxford University Press, 2000.

Joseph Rothblat, ed. *World Citizenship: Allegiance to Humanity.* St. Martin's Press, 1997.

Jonathan Schell. *The Unconquerable World: Power, Nonviolence, and the Will of the People.* Henry Holt and Company, Metropolitan Books, 2003.

Donald Senior and Carroll Stuhlmueller. *The Biblical Foundations for Mission.* Orbis Books, 1983.

Gene Sharp. *The Politics of Nonviolent Action.* 3 vols. Porter Sargent, 1973.

Richard V. Sidy. *World Diplomacy.* SNS Press, 1992.

Anne-Marie Slaughter. *A New World Order.* Princeton University Press, 2004.

Thomas G. Weiss and Leon Gordenker, eds. *NGOs, the UN and Global Governance.* Lynne Rienner Press, 1996.

Rorden Wilkinson, ed. *The Global Governance Reader.* Routledge: Taylor and Francis Group, 2005.

Lawrence S. Wittner. *Toward Nuclear Abolition: A History of the World Nuclear Disarmament Movement.* Stanford University Press, 2003.

I. William Zartman and J. Lewis Rasmussen, eds. *Peacemaking in International Conflict: Methods and Techniques.* United States Institute of Peace, 1997.

Stephen Zunes, Lester R. Kurtz, and Sarab Beth Asher, eds. *Nonviolent Social Movements: A Geographical Perspective.* Blackwell Publishers, 1999.